Muhammad
The Messenger of Allah

May God Exalt his Mention

Second Edition

Written by:

Abdurrahman al-Sheha

Translated by:

Abdurrahmaan Murad

Edited by:

The Islamic Propagation Office at Rabwah

(www.islamhouse.com)

M. M. AbdusSalam

Abu Ayoub Jerome Boulter

© Abdurahman Abdulkarim Al-Sheha , 2005
King Fahd National Library Cataloging-in-Publication Data

Al-Sheha, Abdulrahman Abdulkarim
    Muhammad der Gesandte des Islam, Friede sei auf ihm.
    / Abdulrahman Abdulkarim Al-Sheha .- Riyadh , 2005

    ..p ; 21cm

    ISBN: 9960-47-471-2

    1- Muhammad, The Prophet of Islam d. 632 - Biography
        I-Title

    239 dc   1426/957

    L.D. no. 1426/957
    ISBN: 9960-47-471-2

محمد رسول الله (ﷺ)

عبد الرحمن الشيحة

المترجم: عبد الرحمن مراد

مراجعة:

المكتّب التعاوني للدعوة وتوعية الجاليات بالربوة

(www.islamhouse.com)

م. م. عبدالسلام، أبو أيوب جيروم بولتر

من إصدارات:

المكتّب التعاوني للدعوة وتوعية الجاليات بالربوة

Islamic Propagation Office in Rabwah

P.O.Box 29465 RIYADH 11457 – TEL 4454900 – 4916065
FAX: 4970126 - E-Mail: rabwah@islamhouse.com
http://www.islamhouse.com

Second Edition, 1427/2006

Copyright © 2006 Abdurrahman al-Sheha

We would like to express our sincere appreciation to those who contributed to the publication of this book. May Allah reward them for their efforts. If you have any corrections, comments, or questions about this publication, please feel free to contact us at:

en@islamhouse.com

www.islamhouse.com

1427 H

[3787]

Published by:

The Islamic Propagation Office in Rabwah

Tel. +4454900 - 4916065

Email: en@islamhouse.com

www.islamhouse.com

الإصدار الثاني، 2006/1427

إذا كان لديك أي سؤال أو اقتراح أو تصحيح يرجى مراسلتنا على العنوان التالي:

en@islamhouse.com

المكتب التعاوني للدعوة وتوعية الجاليات بالربوة

هاتف: 4454900 – 4916065

البريد الإلكتروني: en@islamhouse.com

عنوان الموقع: www.islamhouse.com

Table of Contents

All praise is due to God, the Lord[1] of the worlds, and may God praise Prophet Muhammad, and render him and his household safe and secure from all evil.

When talking about Prophet Muhammad (ﷺ)[2], one should keep in mind that he is talking about the greatest individual in history. This is not a baseless claim; for the one who reads his biography and learns of his mannerisms and ethics, while keeping aside all preconceived notions, would certainly reach this conclusion. Some fair and just non-Muslims have reached this conclusion as well.

The late Professor Hasan Ali, may God have mercy on him, said in his magazine 'Noor al-Islam' that a Brahmin[3] colleague of his once told him: "I recognize and believe that the Messenger of Islam is the greatest and most mature man in history." Professor Hasan Ali, may God have mercy on him, asked him: "Why do you consider him as the greatest and most mature man?" He replied:

No man possessed the characteristics, mannerisms and ethics that he possessed at one time. He was a king under whom the entire peninsula was unified; yet he was humble. He believed that the dominion belonged to his God alone.

Great riches would come to him, and yet he lived in a state of poverty; fire would not be lit in his house for many days, and he would stay hungry. He was a great leader; he led small numbers into battle against thousands, and yet he would decisively defeat them. He

---

[1] The actual word used in the Qur'an is *Rubb*. There is no proper equivalent for *Rubb* in the English language. It means the Creator, the Fashioner, the Provider, the One upon Whom all creatures depend for their means of subsistence, and the One Who gives life and causes death.

[2] This Arabic term means, "may God praise him and render him safe from all evil."

[3] Brahmin: member of the highest of the four Hindu castes: the priestly caste.

loved peace agreements and would agree to them with a firm heart, even though he had thousands of his brave and courageous Companions by his side. Each Companion was very brave and could confront a thousand enemies alone, while not feeling the least bit intimidated. Yet, the Prophet was kind-hearted, merciful, and did not want to shed a drop of blood. He was deeply concerned about the affairs of the Arabian Peninsula, yet he did not neglect the affairs of his family, household, or the poor and needy. He was keen to disseminate Islam amongst those who had gone astray. In general, he was a man concerned with the betterment and wellbeing of mankind, yet he did not indulge in amassing worldly fortune. He busied himself with the worship of God and loved doings deeds which pleased Him. He never avenged himself on account of personal reasons. He even prayed for his enemies' wellbeing, and would warn them of the punishment of God.

He was an ascetic regarding worldly affairs and would worship God throughout the night. He was the brave and courageous soldier who fought with the sword - and the infallible Prophet - the conqueror who conquered nations and countries. He slept on a mat of hay and a pillow filled with coarse fibers. People crowned him as the Sultan of the Arabs, or King of the Arabian Peninsula, yet his family lived a simple life, even after they received great fortunes; the riches were piled in the Mosque. Fatima[4] complained to him about the strenuous work she did, the grinding stone and water jug which she used to carry - how they had left marks on her body... He did not give her a portion of that wealth; instead, the Prophet (ﷺ) taught her a few words and supplications. His Companion Umar[5] came to his house and looked in his room, and saw nothing but a hay mat which the Prophet was sitting on, which had left marks on his body. The only provisions in the house were half a *Saa'*[6] of barley in a container, and a water skin that hung on the wall - this is all

---

[4] Fatimah was one of the daughters of the Prophet, may God praise him.

[5] One of the Prophet's close companions, and the second Caliph after his death.

[6] Saa': a measure of capacity equal to four handfuls of the two hands held together.

the Messenger of God owned at a time when half the Arabs were under his control. When Umar saw this, he could not control himself and wept. The Messenger of God (ﷺ) said:

"Why are you weeping O Umar?" He replied: "Why shouldn't I weep - Khosrau and Caesar enjoy themselves in this world and the Messenger of God (ﷺ) only owns what I see!" He responded: "O Umar, wouldn't it please you that this is the share of Khosrau and Caesar in this life, and in the Hereafter this pleasure would be for us alone?"

When the Prophet examined his troops prior to the occupation of Makkah, Abu Sufyan stood beside al-Abbas, the uncle of the Prophet (ﷺ) and they looked at the banners of the Muslim army. Abu Sufyan at that time was not a Muslim. He was amazed by the vast number of Muslims; they advanced towards Makkah like a torrent of water. No one could stop them and nothing stood in their way. Abu Sufyan then said to al-Abbas: 'O Abbas, your nephew has become a grand King!' al-Abbas responded saying: 'This is not kingship, rather prophethood, and the Message of Islam.'

A'dee at-Ta'ee, the son of Ha'tim at-Ta'ee who is the paradigm of generosity, attended the assembly of the Prophet (ﷺ) while he was still a Christian. When he saw how the Companions aggrandized and respected the Prophet (ﷺ), he was confused - was he a Prophet or a king? He asked himself, "Is he a king or a Messenger of the Messengers of God?" While he was pondering over this, a destitute woman came to the Prophet (ﷺ) and said: "I wish to tell you a secret." He said to her: "In which road in Madeenah do you want me to meet you?' The Prophet (ﷺ) left with the destitute maid and took care of her needs. When Ad'ee saw the humbleness of the Prophet (ﷺ), he realized the truth and discarded the crosses that he was wearing and became a Muslim.

We will mention some statements of the Orientalists concerning Muhammad (ﷺ). We as Muslims firmly believe in the Prophet (ﷺ) and his Message, and as such, do not need the statements of non-Muslims to establish this fact. We are mentioning these statements for the following two reasons:

a. To serve as a reminder and admonition for name-sake Muslims who have abandoned their Prophet and his teachings, so that they would heed and return to their religion.[7]

b. So that non-Muslims would know who the Prophet is from the statements of their own people, so that they would be guided to Islam.

I ask all readers to not hold any preconceived notions when searching for the truth, whether it be this or any other Islamic material. I ask God to open their hearts and chests to accept the truth, and to show them the right path and inspire them to follow it.

Abdurrahmaan b. Abdul-Kareem al-Sheha

Riyadh, 11535 P.O. Box 59565

Email: alsheha@yahoo.com

http://www.islamland.org

---

[7] The word translated as religion is *'Deen'*, which in Arabic commonly refers to a way of life, which is both private and public. It is an inclusive term meaning: acts of worship, political practice, and a detailed code of conduct, including hygiene or etiquette matters.

Who is the Messenger, Muhammad (ﷺ)?

His Lineage

He is Abul-Qasim (father of Al-Qasim) Muhammad, the son of Abdullah, the son of Abdul-Mutalib. His lineage traces back to the tribe of Adnan, the son of Ishmael [the Prophet of God, the son of Ibraheem (Abraham)] may God praise them all. His mother is Aminah, the daughter of Wahb.

The Prophet (ﷺ) said:

> 'Indeed God chose the tribe of Kinanah over other tribes from the children of Ishmael; He chose Quraish over other tribes of Kinanah; He chose Banu Hashim over the other families of the Quraish; and He chose me from Banu Hashim.' (Muslim #2276)

Thus, the Prophet (ﷺ) has the noblest lineage on earth. Even his enemies attested to this fact, as did Abu Sufyan, the arch enemy of Islam before he became Muslim, in front of Heraclius[8], the Emperor of Rome.

Abdullah b. Abbas, the nephew of the Prophet, reported that the Messenger of God (ﷺ) wrote to Heraclius and invited him to Islam though a letter he sent with a companion of his named Dihya al-Kalbi. Dihya handed this letter to the Governor of Busra who then forwarded it to Heraclius.

---

[8] He was the Emperor of the Byzantine Empire (610–641) who captured Syria, Palestine, and Egypt from Persia (613–628).

Heraclius, as a sign of gratitude to God, had walked from *Hims* to *Ilya* (i.e. Jerusalem) when God had granted Him victory over the Persian forces. When the letter of the Messenger of God reached Heraclius, he said after reading it, **"Seek for me anyone of his people, (Arabs of the Quraish tribe) if present here, in order to ask him about the Messenger of God!"** At that time Abu Sufyan bin Harb was in *Shaam* (the Greater Syria Area)[9] with some men from Quraish who had come as merchants during the truce that had been concluded between the Messenger of God and the pagans of Quraish. Abu Sufyan said,

"Heraclius' messenger found us somewhere in the Greater Syria area, so he took me and my companions to *Ilya* and we were admitted into Heraclius' presence. We found him sitting in his royal court wearing a crown, surrounded by the senior Byzantine dignitaries. He said to his translator. 'Ask them whom amongst them is a close relation to the man who claims to be a prophet.' "

Abu Sufyan added,

"I replied: 'I am the nearest relative to him.' He asked, 'What degree of relationship do you have with him?' I replied, 'He is my cousin,' and there was none from the tribe of *Abd Manaf* in the caravan except myself. Heraclius said, 'Let him come nearer.' He then ordered that my companions stand behind me near my shoulder

---

[9] This is a historic region in the Middle East bordering the Mediterranean. It is generally considered to include the modern states of Syria, Lebanon, Palestine, and Jordon.

and said to his translator, 'Tell his companions that I am going to ask this man about the one who claims to be a prophet. If he tells a lie, they should contradict him immediately.' "

Abu Sufyan added,

"By God! Had it not been for shame that my companions brand me a liar, I would not have spoken the truth about him when he asked me. But I considered it shameful to be called a liar by my companions, so I told the truth."

"He then said to his translator, 'Ask him what kind of family he belongs to.' I replied, 'He belongs to a noble family amongst us.' He said, 'Has anybody else amongst you ever claimed the same before him?' I replied, 'No.' He said, 'Have you ever blamed him for telling lies before he claimed what he claimed?' I replied, 'No.' He said, 'Was anybody amongst his ancestors a king?' I replied, 'No.' He said, 'Do the noble or the poor follow him?' I replied, 'It is the poor who follow him.' He said, 'Are they increasing or decreasing (daily)?' I replied, 'They are increasing.' He said, 'Does anybody amongst those who embrace his religion become displeased and then discard his religion?' I replied, 'No.' He said, 'Does he break his promises?' I replied, 'No, but we are now at truce with him and we are afraid that he may betray us.'

Abu Sufyan added,

"Other than the last sentence, I could not say anything against him."

"Heraclius then asked, 'Have you ever had a war with him?' I replied, 'Yes.' He said, 'What was the outcome of your battles with him?' I replied, 'Sometimes he was victorious and sometimes we.' He said, 'What does he order you to do?' I said, 'He tells us to worship God alone, and not to worship others along with Him, and to leave all that our fore-fathers used to worship. He orders us to pray, give in charity, be chaste, keep promises and return what is entrusted to us.' "

"When I had said that, Heraclius said to his translator, 'Say to him: I asked you about his lineage and your reply was that he belonged to a noble family. In fact, all the Messengers came from the noblest lineage of their nations. Then I questioned you whether anybody else amongst you had claimed such a thing, and your reply was in the negative. If the answer had been in the affirmative, I would have thought that this man was following a claim that had been said before him. When I asked you whether he was ever blamed for telling lies, your reply was in the negative, so I took it for granted that a person who did not tell a lie to people could never tell a lie about God. Then I asked you whether any of his ancestors was a king. Your reply was in the negative, and if it had been in the affirmative, I would have thought that this man wanted to take back his ancestral kingdom. When I asked you whether the rich or the poor people followed him, you replied that it was the poor who followed him. In fact, such are the followers of the Messengers. Then I asked you whether his followers were increasing or decreasing. You replied that they were increasing. In fact, this is the result of true faith till it is complete [in all respects]. I asked you whether there was anybody who, after embracing his religion, became displeased and discarded his religion; your reply was in the negative. In fact, this is the sign of true faith, for when its pleasure enters and mixes in the hearts completely; nobody will be displeased with it. I asked you whether he had ever broken his promise. You replied in the negative. And such are the Messengers; they never break their promises. When I asked you whether you fought with him and he fought with you, you replied that he did and that sometimes he was victorious and sometimes you. Indeed, such are the Messengers; they are put to trials and the final victory is always theirs. Then I asked you what he ordered you. You replied that he ordered you to worship God alone and not to worship others along with Him, to leave all that your fore-fathers used to worship, to offer prayers, to speak the truth, to be chaste, to keep promises, and to return what is entrusted to you. These are really the qualities of a prophet who, I knew [from the previous Scriptures] would appear, but I did not know that he would be from amongst you. If what you say is true, he will very soon occupy the earth under my feet, and if I knew that I would reach him definitely, I would go immediately to meet him; and were I with him, then I would certainly wash his feet.' "

Abu Sufyan added,

"Heraclius then asked for the letter of the Messenger of God and it was read. Its contents were the following:

I begin with the name of God, the most Beneficent, the most Merciful [This letter is] from Muhammad, the slave of God, and His Messenger, to Heraclius, the Ruler of the Byzantine. Peace be upon the followers of guidance. I invite you to Islam [i.e. surrender to God]). Accept Islam and you will be safe; accept Islam and God will bestow on you a double reward. But if you reject this invitation of Islam, you shall be responsible for misguiding the peasants [i.e. your nation].

❴O people of the Scriptures! Come to a word common between you and us, that we worship God, and that we associate nothing in worship with Him; and that none of us shall take others as Gods besides God. Then if they turn away, say: Bear witness that we are they who have surrendered [unto Him].❵ (3:64)

Abu Sufyan added,

"When Heraclius had finished his speech, there was a great hue and cry caused by the Byzantine dignitaries surrounding him, and there was so much noise that I did not understand what they said. So, we were ordered out of the court."

"When I went out with my companions and we were alone, I said to them, 'Verily, *Ibn Abi Kabsha's* (i.e. the Prophet's) affair has gained power. This is the King of the Romans fearing him.' "

Abu Sufyan added:

"By God, I became surer and surer that his religion would be victorious till I ended up accepting Islam."
(Bukhari #2782)

Place of Birth and Childhood

The Prophet (ﷺ) was born in the year 571 C.E. into the tribe of Quraish [held noble by all Arabs], in Makkah [the religious capital of the Arabian Peninsula].

The Arabs would perform pilgrimage to Makkah and circumambulate the Ka'bah which was built by Prophet Abraham and his son, Prophet Ishmael, may God praise them both.

The Prophet (ﷺ) was an orphan. His father passed away before he was born, and his mother died when he was six years old. He was taken under the care of his grandfather, Abdul-Muttalib, and when he died, his uncle, Abu Talib, took charge of him. His tribe, as well as others, worshipped idols made from stone, wood and even gold. Some of these idols were placed around the Ka'bah. People believed that these idols could ward off harm or extend benefit.

The Prophet (ﷺ) was a trustworthy and honest person. He never behaved treacherously, nor did he lie or cheat; he was known amongst his people as *'Al-Ameen'*, or 'The Trustworthy'. People would entrust him with their valuables when they wanted to travel. He was also known as *'As-Sadiq'* or 'The Truthful' for he never told a lie. He was well-mannered, well-spoken, and he loved to help people. His people loved and revered him and he had beautiful manners. God, the Exalted, says:

《Indeed you are of a great moral character.》 [68:4]

The famous Scottish historian and writer, **Thomas Carlyle** (d. 1885) wrote in his book: *'Heroes, Hero-Worship and the Heroic in History'*:

But, from an early age, he had been remarked as a thoughtful man. His companions named him *"Al Amin, The Faithful."* A man of truth and fidelity; true in what he did, in what he spoke and thought. They noted that he always meant something. A man rather taciturn in speech; silent when there was nothing to be said; but pertinent, wise, sincere, when he did speak; always throwing light on the matter. This is the only sort of speech worth speaking! Through life we find him to have been regarded as an altogether solid, brotherly, genuine man. A serious, sincere character; yet amiable, cordial, companionable, jocose even - a good laugh in him withal: there are men whose laugh is as untrue as anything about them; who cannot laugh. A spontaneous, passionate, yet just, true-meaning man! Full of wild faculty, fire and light; of wild worth, all uncultured; working out his life - takes in the depth of the Desert there.

The Prophet (صلى الله عليه وسلم) liked to seclude himself in the Cave of *Hira* before he was commissioned as a prophet. He would stay there many nights at a time.

He (صلى الله عليه وسلم) never partook in any falsehood; he never drank intoxicants, nor did he ever bow to a statue or idol, take an oath by them or offer to them an offering. He was a shepherd over a flock of sheep which belonged to his people. The Prophet (صلى الله عليه وسلم) said:

'Every prophet commissioned by God was a shepherd over a flock of sheep.' His companions asked him: 'Even you, O Messenger of God?' He said: 'Yes, I would take care of a flock of sheep for the people of Makkah.' (Bukhari 2143)

At the age of forty, the Prophet (ﷺ) received divine revelation when at the cave of Hira. The Mother of the believers, A'ishah[10] said:

The first thing that God's Messenger (ﷺ) received while in the Cave of *Hira* in Makkah were good visions [dreams]. Every time he had a dream, it would come true and clear like the split of the dawn. Later on, God's Messenger (ﷺ) began to love being alone in meditation. He spent lengthy periods for days and nights to fulfill this purpose in the cave before returning back to his family. He would take a supply of food for his trip. When he came back to his wife Khadeejah[11] he would get a fresh supply of food and go back to the same cave to continue his meditation.

The Truth came to him while he was in the Cave of *Hira*. The Angel Gabriel came to Muhammad (ﷺ) and commanded him to read. Muhammad (ﷺ) replied, "I cannot read!" Gabriel embraced Muhammad (ﷺ) until he could not breathe, and then let him go saying, "O Muhammad! Read!" Again, Muhammad (ﷺ) replied, "I cannot read!" Gabriel embraced Muhammad (ﷺ) for the second time. He

---

[10] A wife of the Prophet (ﷺ).

[11] Khadeejah was the first wife of the Prophet.

then ordered him to read for the third time, when he did not he embraced him tightly until he could not breathe, and then released him saying, "O Muhammad!

❮Recite with the Name of Your Lord Who has created (all that exists). He has created man out of a (mere) clot of congealed blood: Read! And your Lord is the Most Generous.❯(96:1-3)

The Messenger of God (ﷺ) returned home trembling. He entered his home and told Khadeejah: "Cover me up, cover me up!" Khadeejah covered Muhammad (ﷺ) until he felt better. He then informed her about what happened to him in the Cave of *Hira*. He said, "I was concerned about myself and my well-being." Khadeejah assured Muhammad (ﷺ) saying:

By God! You don't have to worry! God, the Exalted, will never humiliate you! You are good to your kith and kin. You help the poor and needy. You are generous and hospitable to your guests. You help people who are in need.

Khadeejah took her husband Muhammad (ﷺ) to a cousin of hers named Waraqah bin Nawfal bin Asad bin Abdul Uzza. This man became a Christian during the pre-Islamic times, known as the Era of Ignorance. He was a scribe, who wrote the Scripture in Hebrew. He was an old man who became blind at the latter part of his life. Khadeejah said to her cousin,

"O cousin, listen to what your nephew [i.e. Muhammad ﷺ] is about to tell you!" Waraqah said: "What is it you have seen, dear nephew?"

The Messenger of God (ﷺ) informed him of what he had seen in the Cave of *Hira.* Upon hearing his report, Waraqah said,

"By God! This is the Angel Gabriel who came to Prophet Moses, may God praise him. I wish I would be alive when your people will drive you out of Makkah!" The Messenger of God (ﷺ) wondered: "Are they going to drive me out of Makkah?!" Waraqah affirmed positively saying, "Never has a man conveyed a Message similar to what you have been charged with, except that his people waged war against him - if I am to witness this, I will support you."

Waraqah lived only a short period after this incident and passed away. Revelation also stopped for a while.' (Bukhari #3)

The chapter of the Qur'an quoted in the hadeeth[12] above marks the beginning when he was commissioned as a Prophet. God, the Exalted, then revealed to him:

⟨O you (Muhammad ﷺ) enveloped (in garments); Arise and warn! And your Lord (Allah) magnify! And your garments purify!⟩ (74:1-4)

---

[12] The narration of a statement, deed, tacit approval, or characteristic of the Prophet.

This chapter of the Qur'an marks the beginning when he was commissioned as a Messenger.

With the revelation of this chapter of the Qur'an, the Prophet (ﷺ) began calling his nation to Islam openly. He began with his own people. Some of them refused adamantly to listen to him, for to them, he was calling to a matter which they had never witnessed before.

The religion of Islam is a complete way of life, which deals with religious, political, economical and social affairs. Furthermore, the religion of Islam did not only call them to worship God alone and to forsake all idols and things they worshipped; rather, it prohibited them from things they considered pleasurable, such as consuming interest and intoxicants, fornication, and gambling. It also called people to be just and fair with one another, and to know that there was no difference between them except through piety. How could the Quraish [the most noble tribe amongst the Arabs] stand to be treated equally with the slaves! They did not only adamantly refuse to accept Islam; rather, they harmed him and blamed him, saying that he was crazy, a sorcerer and a liar. They blamed him with things they would dare not have before the advent of Islam. They incited the ignorant masses against him, harmed him and tortured his companions. Abdullah b. Masood, a close companion of the Prophet said:

> While the Prophet (ﷺ) was standing up and praying near the Ka'bah, a group of Quraish were sitting in their sitting place, one of them said: "Do you see this man? Would someone bring the dirt and filth and

25

bloody intestines from the camels of so and so, and wait till he prostrates, and then place it between his shoulders?" The most wretched amongst them volunteered to do it, and when the Prophet (囊) prostrated, he put the filth between his shoulders, so the Prophet (囊) stayed in prostration. They laughed so hard that they were about to fall on each other. Someone went to Fatimah who was a young girl, and informed her of what had happened. She hurriedly came towards the Prophet (囊) and removed the filth from his back, and then she turned around and she cursed the Quraishites who were sitting in that sitting. (Bukhari #498)

Muneeb al-Azdi, a companion of the Prophet (囊) said:

I saw the Messenger of God in the Era of Ignorance saying to people: "Say there is no god worthy of being worshipped except Allah if you would be successful." There were those who spat in his face, those who threw soil in his face, and those who swore at him until midday. When [once] a certain young girl came with a big container of water, he washed his face and hands and say: "O daughter, do not fear that your father will be humiliated or struck by poverty." (Mu'jam al-Kabeer # 805)

Abdullah b. Amr al-Aas, a companion of the Prophet (囊) was asked about some of the evil the pagans did to the Prophet (囊), to which he replied:

[Once a pagan] approached the Prophet (囊) while he was praying near the Ka'bah and twisted his garment around his neck. Abu Bakr[13] hurriedly approached and grabbed his shoulder and pushed him away saying: "Do you kill a man because he proclaims Allah as his Lord, and clear signs have come to you from your Lord?" (Bukhari 3643)

These incidents did not stop the Prophet (ﷺ) from calling to Islam. He preached this message to the many tribes that came to Makkah for Hajj[14]. A few believed from the people of Yathrib (a small city north of Makkah), known today as Madeenah, and they pledged to support him and help him if he chose to migrate there. He sent with them Mus'ab b. Umair to teach them the tenets of Islam. After all the hardships that the Muslims of Makkah faced from their own people, God granted them the permission to migrate to Madeenah. The people of Madeenah greeted them and received them in a most extraordinary manner. Madeenah became the capital of the new Islamic state, and the place from which the call to Islam was spread far and wide.

The Prophet (ﷺ) settled there and taught people how to recite the Qur'an and the rulings of the religion. The inhabitants of Madeenah were greatly moved and touched by the Prophet's manners. They loved him more than they loved their own selves; they would rush to serve him, and they would spend all they had in the path of Islam. The society was strong and its people were rich in Faith, and they were extremely happy. People loved each other, and

---

[13] The closest companion to the Prophet (ﷺ) and the first Caliph of Islam after his death.

[14] Pilgrimage to Makkah.

true brotherhood was apparent amongst its people. All people were equal; the rich, noble and poor, black and white, Arab and non-Arab - they were all considered as equals in the religion of God, no distinction was made among them except through piety. After the Quraish learnt that the Prophet's call had spread, they fought him in the first battle in Islam, the Battle of Badr. This battle took place between two groups unequal in preparations and weapons. The Muslims numbered 314; whereas, the pagans were 1000 strong. God gave victory to the Prophet (ﷺ) and the Companions. After this battle, a number of battles took place between the Muslims and the pagans. After eight years, the Prophet (ﷺ) was able to prepare an army 10,000 strong. They proceeded towards Makkah and conquered it, and with this Muhamamad (ﷺ) overcame the people who had harmed and tortured him and his Companions with every conceivable cruelty. In their fleeing for their lives, they had even been forced to leave their property and wealth behind. The year of this decisive victory is called 'The Year of the Conquest.' Allah, the Exalted, says:

❨When the victory of Allah has come and the conquest, and you see the people entering into the religion of Allah in multitudes, then glorify the Praises of your Lord and ask His forgiveness. Indeed, He is the One Who accepts the repentance and Who forgives.❩
[110:1-3]

Upon the conquest, the Prophet (ﷺ) gathered the people of Makkah and said to them:

"What do you think I will do to you?" They answered: "You will only do something favorable; you are a kind and generous brother, and a kind and generous nephew!" The Prophet (繋) said: "Go - you are free." (Baihaqi #18055)

This incredible act of forgiveness caused many to accept Islam. The Prophet (繋) then returned to Madeenah. After a period of time, the Prophet (繋) intended to perform Hajj, so he headed towards Makkah with 114,000 Companions and performed Hajj. This Hajj is known as 'Hajjatul-Wadaa' or the 'Farewell Pilgrimage' since the Prophet (繋) never performed another Hajj, and died shortly after he performed it.

On the 9th of Dhul-Hijjah at Mount Arafat, the Prophet (繋), delivered his farewell sermon. After praising Allah, he said:

O People! Lend me an attentive ear, for I know not whether after this year, I shall ever be amongst you again. Therefore listen to what I am saying to you very carefully and take these words to those who could not be present here today.

O People! Just as you regard this month, this day, this city as sacred, so regard the life and property of every Muslim. Return the goods entrusted to you to their rightful owners. Hurt no one so that no one may hurt you. Remember, you will indeed meet your Lord and He will indeed reckon your deeds. Allah has forbidden you to take usury; therefore all interest obligation shall henceforth be waived. Your capital, however, is yours to keep. You will neither inflict nor suffer inequity. Beware of Satan for the safety of your religion. He has lost all hope that he will ever be able to lead you astray in great things, so beware of following him in small things.

O People! It is true that you have certain rights with regards to your women, but they also have rights over you. Remember that you have taken them as your wives only under Allah's trust and with His permission. If they abide by your right, then to them belongs the right to be fed and clothed in kindness. Do treat your women well and be kind to them, for they are your partners and committed helpers. And it is your right that they do not take as intimate friends those whom you do not approve of as well as to never be unchaste.

O People! Listen to me in earnest; worship Allah, perform your five daily prayers, fast the month of Ramadhan, give alms and perform the pilgrimage (i.e. Hajj) if you can afford to. All mankind is from Adam and Adam is from clay. There is no superiority for an Arab over a non-Arab, nor for a non-Arab over an Arab; or for a white over a black, nor for a black over a white; except through piety. Know that every Muslim is a brother to every other Muslim and that the Muslims are one community. Nothing shall be legitimate to a Muslim that belongs to another unless it was given freely and willingly. Do not, therefore, do injustice to yourselves.

Remember, one day you will appear before Allah and answer for your deeds. So beware! Do not stray from the path of righteousness after I am gone. O People! No prophet or messenger will come after me and no new faith will be born. Reason well, therefore, O people! And understand the words that I convey to you. I leave behind me two things, if you follow them you will never go astray: the Book of Allah (i.e. the Qur'an) and my Sunnah. All those who listen to me shall pass on my words to others and those to others again; and may the last ones understand my words better than those who listen to me directly. Be my witness, O Allah, that I have conveyed Your Message to Your People.'

The Prophet (ﷺ) died in Madeenah on the 12th day of Rabi al-Awal in the 11th year of Hijrah and was buried there as well. The Muslims were shocked when they learnt of his death; some Companions did not believe it. Umar said: 'Whoever says that Muhammad is dead, I will behead him!' Abu Bakr then addressed the Muslims and read the words of God:

❰Muhammad is not but a Messenger. Other messengers have passed away before him. So if he was to die or be killed, would you turn back on your heels to unbelief? And He who turns back on his heels will never harm God at all; but God will reward the grateful.❱ [3:144]

When Umar heard this verse, he stopped saying what he was saying, since he was very keen on applying the rules of God. The Prophet (ﷺ) was 63 years of age when he died.

The Prophet (ﷺ) stayed in Makkah for forty years before being commissioned as a Prophet. After being commissioned as a Prophet; he lived there for another thirteen years, in which he called people to the pure monotheistic belief of Islam. He then migrated to Madeenah, and stayed there for ten years. He continued to receive revelation there, until the Qur'an and the religion of Islam were complete.

The famous playwright and critic, George Bernard Shaw (d. 1950) said:

I have always held the religion of Muhammad in high estimation because of its wonderful vitality. It is the only religion which appears to possess that assimilating capability to the changing phases of existence which make itself appeal to every age - I have prophesized about the faith of Muhammad that it would be acceptable tomorrow as it is beginning to be acceptable to the Europe of today. Medieval ecclesiastics, either through ignorance or bigotry, painted Muhammadanism in the darkest colours. They were, in fact, trained to hate both the man Muhammad and his religion. To them, Muhammad was an anti-Christ. I have studied him, the wonderful man, and in my opinion, far from being an anti-Christ, he must be called the Saviour of humanity.[15]

---

[15] Encyclopedia of Seerah, by Afzalur Rahman.

The Description of the Prophet (ﷺ)

The Prophet was of a slightly above-average height. Amazingly, in gatherings, he would appear taller than those actually taller than him - until the people dispersed. In complexion, he was white with a rosy tinge; pale, but not excessively so. His hair was jet black and wavy, but stopped short of curling, and was kept between his ear-lobes and shoulders. Sometimes he would part his hair at the middle. Other times, he would wear it braided. The Prophet (ﷺ) had the physique of a powerful man. He had a broad upper-back and shoulders between which was the Seal of Prophethood. He had long muscular limbs, large joints and a wide girth. His lean stomach never protruded out past the profile of his chest. His face was radiant, "as if the sun were following its course across and shining from his face," said one Companion. His neck was silvery white; his forehead, prominent; his pupils, large and black; his eyelashes, long and thick; his nose, high-tipped with narrow nostrils. At the time of his death, the Prophet had exactly 17 white hairs shared between his temples and the front of his thick, beard. He had hair on his forearms and shins and a line of fine hair also ran from his chest to his navel.

The Prophet (ﷺ) would walk briskly with a forward-leaning gait, moving with strength of purpose and lifting each foot clearly off the ground. His pace was such that fit men would tire trying to keep up. When he turned, he would turn his whole body, giving full attention to the one addressing him and showing complete concern to what was being said. When he pointed, he would use an open hand so as not to offend. Likewise, when he criticized a person's behavior, rather than name the individual, he would simply say: "Why do people do so and so?" He would laugh only to the extent that the gap between his front teeth would become visible. He would become angry only to the extent that his face would turn red and the vein between his fine, bow-shaped eyebrows would bulge. He once said:

"I am the master of the descendants of Adam and I do not say so out of pride." (Tirmidthi)

That freedom from pride was obvious even to children, who would playfully lead the Prophet (ﷺ) through the streets of Medina whilst grasping his finger. Indeed he had said:

"He who does not show mercy to our young, nor honor our old, is not from us." (Abu Dawood)

{(Allah has sent you) a Messenger who recites to you the clear Signs of Allah that He may take out those who believe and work righteousness from the darkness to the light (of Islamic Monotheism). } [65:11]

Ali, cousin and son-in-law to the Prophet, said of Muhammad:

'He was the Last of the Prophets, the most giving of hearts, the most truthful, the best of them in temperament and the most sociable. Whoever unexpectedly saw him would stand in awe of him, and whoever accompanied him and got to know him would love him. Those describing him would say: "I have never seen anyone before or after him who was comparable to him."

The Prophet's beloved wife, A'ishah, said of her selfless husband:

"He always joined in household chores and would at times mend his clothes, repair his shoes and sweep the floor. He would milk, tether and feed his animals."

(Bukhari)

She also described his character as: "The Qur'an (exemplified).'

《Indeed in the Messenger of Allah you have an excellent example to follow for whoever hopes in Allah and the Last Day and remembers Allah much.》 [33:21]

Some of the Prophet's Manners and Characteristics:

1. **Sound Intellect**: The Messenger (ﷺ) had an excellent, complete and sound intellect. No man has ever had an intellect as complete and perfect as his. Qadhi Iyaadh[16], may God have mercy on him, said:

> This becomes clear to an individual when the researcher reads the Prophet's biography and understands his state of affairs, and his meaningful and inclusive utterances and traditions, his good manners, ethics and moral character, his knowledge of the Torah and Gospel and other Divine Scriptures, and his knowledge of statements of the wise, and knowledge of bygone nations, and ability to strike examples and implement policies and correct emotional manners. He was an example and paradigm to which his people could relate to in all branches of knowledge; acts of worship, medicine, laws of inheritance, lineage, and other matters as well. He knew and learned all of this without reading or examining the Scriptures of those before us, nor did he sit with their scholars. The Prophet had no formal schooling, and was without knowledge of the above before being commissioned as a Prophet, nor could he read or write. The Prophet (ﷺ) was wise to the fullest extent of his mental capacity. God, the Exalted, informed him of some of

---

[16] A great scholar of Islam who wrote many works, including on the Biography of the Prophet (ﷺ).

what had taken place (in the past) and of that which would take place in the future. This is a sign that the Dominion belongs to God, and that He is capable over all things.[17]

2. **Doing Things for the Sake of God:** The Prophet (ﷺ) would always do deeds through which he would seek the pleasure of God. He was harmed and abused when he invited and called people to Islam; yet he was patient and endured all of this, and hoped for the reward of God. Abdullah b. Masood said:

'The Prophet (ﷺ) resembled a prophet who was harmed by his people. He wiped the blood from his face and said: 'O God! Forgive my people, for they know not!' (Bukhari #3290)

Jundub b. Sufyaan said that the Messenger's finger bled during one of the battles, and he said:

'You are but a finger which has bled; which suffers in the path of God.' (Bukhari #2648)

3. **Sincerity:** The Prophet (ﷺ) was sincere and honest in all his matters, as God had ordered him. Allah, the Exalted, says:

❴Say, 'Indeed, my prayer, my rites of sacrifice, my living and my dying are for God, Lord of the worlds. No partner has He. And this I have been commanded and I am the first (among you) of the Muslims.❵ [6:162-163]

---

[17] Qadhi Eiyadh, *'Al-Shifa bita'reefi Hoquooqil-Mostafa'*

4. **Good Morals, Ethics and Companionship**: The Prophet (ﷺ) was a living example for all humans to follow. His wife A'ishah was asked about his manners, and she said,

'His manners were the Qur'an.'

In this statement, A'ishah meant that the Prophet (ﷺ) abided by its laws and commands and abstained from its prohibitions, and observed the virtuous deeds mentioned in it. The Prophet (ﷺ) said:

'God has sent me to perfect good manners and to do good deeds.' (Bukhari & Ahmed)

Allah, the Exalted, described the Prophet (ﷺ) saying:

《And indeed, you are of a great moral character》 [68:4]

Anas b. Malik served the Prophet (ﷺ) for ten years; He was with him day in and day out, both when the Prophet (ﷺ) traveled and when he was a resident in Madeenah. He was knowledgeable of the Prophet's manners. He said:

'The Prophet (ﷺ) did not swear at anyone, nor was he rude, nor did he curse anyone. If he desired to reprimand someone, he would say: 'What is wrong with him, may dust be cast in his face!' (Bukhari #5684)

5. **Politeness and Good Manners**: The Prophet (ﷺ) showed good manners and was courteous to all, even to children. Once when the Prophet was in a gathering, a drink was brought to the Prophet (ﷺ) and he drank from it. On his right side there was a young boy and on his left side were elderly men. Feeling obliged by the respect of

elders, and not wanting to hurt the feelings of the child, he asked the young boy:

'Do you mind if I give the drink to them?' The young boy said: 'O Prophet of God! By God! I would not prefer anyone to drink from the place you drank. This is my fair share[18].' The Messenger of God (ﷺ) handed the boy the drink." (Bukhari #2319)

6. **Love for Reformation and Reconciliation:** Whenever a situation occurred which called for reconciliation, the Prophet (ﷺ) would hurry to resolve it. Once when he heard that the people of *Qubaa'*[19] disputed with each other about a matter, the Prophet (ﷺ) said:

'Let us go to resolve the situation and make peace between them.' (Bukhari #2547)

7. **Ordering with the good and forbidding evil:** If the Prophet (ﷺ) saw an act which opposed a tenet of the religion, he would reprimand it in a suitable manner. Abdullah b. Abbas said:

The Messenger of God ﷺ saw a man wearing a gold ring[20], so he reached for it, [and] removed it…. He then said:

'Would one of you seek a burning charcoal and place it on his hand?!'

---

[18] According to Islamic etiquette. One should always begin from the right.

[19] A town previously on the outskirts of Madeenah.

[20] It is prohibited for men to wear gold in Islam.

The man was later told, after the Prophet 🕊 left: 'Take your ring! Make good use of it [by selling it].' The man said: 'No, by God! I will never take it after the Messenger of God 🕊 cast it away.' (Muslim #2090)

Abu Saeed al-Khudri said: 'I heard the Messenger of Allah say: 'Whoever of you sees an evil action, let him change it with his hand; and if he is not able to do so, then with his tongue; and if he is not able to do so, then with his heart...' (Muslim)

8. **Love of Purification**: A companion passed by the Prophet (🕊) while he was not in a state of purification. He greeted him with God's name, but the Prophet (🕊) did not return the greeting until he performed ablution and apologized saying:

'I disliked that I should mention God's name while I am not in a state of purity.' (Ibn Khuzaimah #206)

9. **Safeguarding and Minding One's Language**: The Messenger of God (🕊) would busy himself with the remembrance of God; he would not talk in vain. He would lengthen his prayers and shorten the speech, and he would not hesitate to help and take care of the needs of a needy, poor or widow. (Ibn Hib'ban #6423)

10. **Excelling in Acts of Worship**: A'ishah said that the Prophet of God (🕊) used to pray during the night until his feet would swell. She said, 'Why do you do this, O Mes-

senger of God, while God has forgiven your past and future sins?' The Prophet (ﷺ) replied:

'Shall I not be a grateful slave (of God)?' (Bukhari #4557)

11. **Forbearance**: Once some companions came to the Prophet (ﷺ) complaining about a tribe, namely the *Daws*, who refused to accept Islam, asking him to curse them. The Prophet (ﷺ) raised his hands in prayer and instead said:

'O Allah guide the tribe of *Daws* and bring them to Islam!'

12. **Good Appearance**: The companions knew the Prophet (ﷺ) to be the most beautiful of people. One companion said:

'The Prophet (ﷺ) was a person of average height. His shoulders were wide. His hair reached his earlobes. Once I saw him adorned in a red garment; I never saw anything more beautiful than him.' (Bukhari #2358)

13. **Asceticism in Worldly Affairs**: There are many examples in the Prophet's life which prove that he had no concern for the pleasures of this life. Abdullah b. Masood said:

'The Messenger of God (ﷺ) went to sleep on a mat. He stood up and he had marks on his side due to the mat that he had slept on. We said: 'O Messenger of God, shall we not make [a proper] bedding for you?'

He said: 'What do I have to do with this world? I am only like a wayfarer upon a mount that stopped to take shade and rest under a tree, and then leaves it behind and continues on the journey.'

(Tirmidthi #2377)

Amr' b. al-Haarith said the Messenger of God (ﷺ) did not leave any gold or silver currency, or a slave, male or female, after his death. He only left behind his white mule, his weapons and a piece of land which he declared as Charity.' (Bukhari #2588)

14. **Altruism:** Sahl b. Sa'd said: The Prophet (ﷺ) had more care for those around him than for his own self.

'A woman gave the Messenger of God (ﷺ) a *Burdah* (gown). The Prophet (ﷺ) asked his Companions: 'Do you know what a *Burdah* is?' They replied, 'Yes, O Prophet of God! It is a piece of woven cloth [similar to a shawl]. The woman said: 'O Prophet of God! I have woven this shawl with my own hands, for you to wear.' The Messenger of God (ﷺ) took it while he direly needed it. After a while, the Messenger of God (ﷺ) came out of his home wearing it, and a Companion said to the Messenger of God (ﷺ): 'O Prophet of God! Grant me this shawl to wear!' The Messenger of God (ﷺ) said: 'Yes.' He then sat for awhile, and headed back home, folded it and gave it to the person who asked for it. The Companions scolded him saying: 'It was not appropriate for you to ask for his shawl; especially since you know he does not turn anyone down or send them away empty-handed! The man said: 'By God! I only asked him to give it to me because I want to be shrouded in this shawl when I die.' Sahl, the narrator of the Hadeeth said: 'The shawl was used as a shroud for that man when he died.' (Bukhari #1987)

15. Strong Faith and Dependence on God: Although the Prophet (ﷺ) and his companions faced severe trials from the disbelievers, he always reminded them that the end was for the believers, and that the Will of God will come to pass. When Abu Bakr and the Prophet hid in a cave after they had left their homes in order to migrate to Madeenah, the disbelievers of Makkah had sent scouts in search of them. They came so close to the cave that Abu Bakr could see their feet. Abu Bakr said:

'I looked at the feet of the pagans while we were in the cave [of *Thawr*]. I said, 'O Prophet of God! If anyone of them looks down at his feet he would see us!' The Messenger of God (ﷺ) said: 'O Abu Bakr! What do you think of two with whom God, the Exalted, is their Third?' (Muslim #1854)

16. Kindness and Compassion: The Prophet was the kindest of people, and this was also apparent in his treatment of infants.

'The Messenger of God (ﷺ) performed *Salah* (prayer) while he was carrying an infant girl named Umaamah, daughter of Abul-Aas. When he bowed, he put her on the ground, and when he stood up, he would carry her again.' (Bukhari #5650)

17. Simplification and Ease: The Prophet (ﷺ) always sought to make things easy for people. The Messenger of God (ﷺ) said:

'I start the prayer with the intention of lengthening it, but when I hear a child crying, I shorten the prayer, as I know its mother would suffer from his screams!' (Bukhari #677)

18. Fearing God, being Mindful to not trespass His Limits: The Messenger of God (ﷺ) said:

'Sometimes, when I return to my family, I would find a date-fruit on the bed. I would pick it up to eat it; but I would fear that it was from the charity[21], and thus, throw it back [on the ground].' (Bukhari #2300)

19. Spending Generously: Anas bin Malik said:

'The Messenger of God (ﷺ) was never asked for something when a person accepted Islam, except that he granted that person what he asked. A man came to the Prophet (ﷺ) and he gave him a herd of sheep that was grazing between two mountains. The man returned to his people and said: 'O my people accept Is-

---

[21] It was forbidden by God for the Prophet (ﷺ) or his family to accept any form of charity.

lam! Muhammad (ﷺ) gives out generously like one who does not fear poverty.' (Muslim #2312)

Ibn Abbas said:

'The Prophet (ﷺ) was the most generous of people. He was most generous during Ramadhan when he met Gabriel (ﷺ); he would meet him every night during Ramadhan to practice and review the Qur'an with him. The Messenger of God (ﷺ) was so generous, that he was faster than the swiftest wind in this regard. (Bukhari #6)

Abu Dharr said:

'I was walking with the Prophet (ﷺ) in the *Har'rah* (volcanic region) of Madeenah and we faced the mount of Uhud; the Prophet (ﷺ) said: 'O Abu Dharr!' I said: 'Here I am O Messenger of God!' He said: 'It would not please me to have an amount of gold equal to the weight of Mount Uhud, until I spend and give it out (in the sake of God) within a night or within three nights. I would keep a single silver piece of it to help those who are in debt. (Bukhari #2312)

Jabir b. Abdullah said:

'The Prophet ﷺ did not refuse to give anything which he had to someone if he asked for it.' (Bukhari #5687)

20. **Cooperation:** The Prophet (ﷺ) was not a king who commanded his followers to carry out his orders. Rather he always carried out his own affairs and helped others in

collective duties. A'ishah was once asked about how the Prophet (ﷺ) behaved with his family. She said:

'He helped and assisted his family members with their chores; but when the call to prayer was heard, he would [stop everything and] leave to attend the prayers.'

Al-Baraa bin 'Azib said:

"I saw the Messenger of God (ﷺ) on the Day of the Trench carrying dirt [that was dug from the trench] until his chest was covered with dirt." (Bukhari #2780)

21. Truthfulness: A'ishah said:

'The trait and characteristic which the Prophet (ﷺ) hated most was lying. A man would tell a lie in the presence of the Prophet (ﷺ) and he would hold it against him, until he knew that he repented.' (Tirmidthi #1973)

Even his enemies attested to his truthfulness. Abu Jahl, who was one of the harshest enemies of Islam, said: 'O Muhammad! I do not say that you are a liar! I only deny what you brought and what you call people to.' God, the Exalted, says:

{We know indeed that what they say certainly grieves you, but surely they do not call you a liar; but the unjust deny the verses of God.} [6:33]

22. Aggrandizing the limits set by Allah, and Always Seeking the Moderate Path: A'ishah said:

'The Prophet (ﷺ) was not given a choice between two matters, except that he chose the easier of the two, as long as it was not a sinful act. If that act was a sinful act, he would be the farthest from it. By God! He never avenged himself. He only became angry when people transgressed the limits and boundaries of God; in that case he avenged [for the sake of God].'
(Bukhari #6404)

23. **Pleasant Facial Expression:** Abdullah bin al-Harith said:

'I have never seen a man who smiled as much as the Messenger of God (ﷺ).' **(Tirmidthi #2641)**

24. **Honesty, Trustworthiness and Reliability:** The Prophet (ﷺ) was well-known for his honesty. The pagans of Makkah -who were openly hostile towards him- would leave their valuables with him. His honesty and reliability was tested when the pagans of Makkah abused him and tortured his companions and drove them out of their homes. He ordered his cousin, Ali b. Abi Talib to postpone his migration for three days to return to people their valuables.[22]

Another example of his honesty, trustworthiness and reliability is demonstrated in the Truce of *Hudaibiyah*, wherein he agreed to the article in the treaty which stated that any man who left the Prophet (ﷺ) would not be returned to him, and any man who left Makkah would be

---

[22] Ibn Hisham's Biography, Vol. 1, p.493 [Arabic Edition].

returned to them. Before the treaty was concluded a man named Abu Jandal b. Amr had managed to escape from the pagans of Makkah and rushed to join Muhammad (ﷺ). The pagans asked Muhammad to honor his pledge and return the escapee. The Messenger of God (ﷺ) said:

'O Abu Jandal! Be patient and ask God to grant you patience. God will surely help you and those who are persecuted and make it easy for you. We have signed an agreement with them, and we certainly do not betray or act treacherously.' (Baihaquee #18611)

25. Bravery and courage: Ali said:

'You should have seen him on the Day of Badr! We sought refuge with the Messenger of God (ﷺ). He was the closest among us to the enemy. On that Day, the Messenger of God (ﷺ) was the strongest one among us.' (Ahmed #654)

As for his courage and bravery under normal circumstances - Anas b. Malik said:

'The Messenger of God (ﷺ) was the best of people and the most courageous. One night, the people of Madeenah were frightened and headed towards the sounds they heard during the night. The Messenger of God (ﷺ) met them while coming back from the place of the sound, after he made sure that there was no trouble. He was riding a horse that belonged to Abu Talhah without any saddle, and he had his sword with him. He was assuring the people, saying:

'Do not be frightened! Do not be frightened!' (Bukhari #2751)

He met up with people riding a horse with no saddle, and he carried his sword, for there might be a reason or need to use it. He did not wait for others to investigate the source of trouble as is usually done in these situations.

26. **Bashfulness and Modesty**: Abu Ayoub al-Ansari said that the Messenger of Allah (ﷺ) said: 'Four (traits) are from the practice of the Messengers; modesty, using perfume and *siwak* (tooth stick) and marriage.' (Tirmidthi)

A'ishah said: 'A woman asked the Prophet (ﷺ) about the bath which is taken at the end of the menstrual period. The Prophet (ﷺ) said: "Purify yourself with a piece of cloth scented with musk." The Prophet (ﷺ) felt shy and turned his face. A'ishah said: "I pulled her to myself and told her what the Prophet (ﷺ) meant."' (Bukhari #313)

27. **Humbleness**: The Messenger of God (ﷺ) was the most humble person. He was so humble that if a stranger were to enter the mosque and approach the Prophet's sitting place while he was sitting with his Companions, one would not be able to distinguish him from his Companions. Anas bin Malik said:

'Once, while we were sitting with the Messenger of God (ﷺ) in the Masjid, a man on his camel approached. After he tied it with a rope, he asked: 'Who amongst you is Muhammad?' The Messenger of God (ﷺ) was sitting on the ground while he was leaning,

49

with his Companions. We directed the Bedouin, saying: 'This white man leaning on the ground.' The Prophet (ﷺ) did not differ nor distinguish himself from his Companions.

The Prophet (ﷺ) would not hesitate to help the poor, needy and widows in their needs. Anas b. Malik said:

'A woman from the people of Madeenah who was partially insane said to the Prophet (ﷺ): 'I have to ask you [your help] about something.' He helped her and took care of her needs.' (Bukhari #670)

28. **Mercy and Compassion**: Abu Masood al-Ansari said:

'A man came to the Prophet (ﷺ) and said: "O Messenger of God! By God! I do not pray Fajr prayer because so and so lengthens the prayer." He said: 'I have never seen the Messenger of God (ﷺ) deliver a speech in such an angry state. He said:

'O People! Verily there are among you those who chase people away! If you lead people in prayer, shorten the prayer. There are old and weak people and those with special needs behind you in prayer.' (Bukhari #670)

Once when the Prophet (ﷺ) went to visit his grandchild he shed some tears.

The Messenger of God (ﷺ) sat with the child while he was on his deathbed. The child's eyes froze in their places like stones. Upon seeing that, the Messenger of God (ﷺ) wept. Sa'd said to him, 'What is this 'O Prophet of God?' He said: 'This is a mercy that God, the Exalted, places in the hearts of His slaves. Truly, God is merciful to those who are merciful towards others.' (Bukhari #6942)

29. Patience and Forbearance: Anas bin Malik said:

'Once, I was walking with the Messenger of God (ﷺ) while he was wearing a Yemeni cloak with a collar with rough edges. A Bedouin grabbed him strongly. I looked at the side of his neck and saw that the edge of the cloak left a mark on his neck. The Bedouin said, 'O Muhammad! Give me [some] of the wealth of God that you have.' The Messenger of God (ﷺ) turned to the Bedouin, laughed and ordered that he be given [some money].' (Bukhari #2980)

Another example of his patience is the story of the Jewish Rabbi, Zaid bin Sa'nah. Zaid had given something as a loan to the Messenger of God (ﷺ). He himself said,

'Two or three days prior to the return of the debt, the Messenger of God (ﷺ) was attending the funeral of a man from the Ansar. Abu Bakr and Umar, Uthman and some other Companions were with the Prophet (ﷺ). After he prayed the funeral prayer he sat down close to a wall, and I came towards him, grabbed him by the edges of his cloak, and looked at him in a harsh way, and said: 'O Muhammad! Will you not pay me back my loan? I have not known the family of Abdul-Mutalib to delay in repaying debts!"

I looked at Umar b. al-Khat'taab - his eyes were swollen with anger! He looked at me and said: 'O Enemy of God, do you talk to the Messenger of God and behave towards him in this manner?! By the One who sent him with the truth, had it not been for the fear of not entering the Heavenly Gardens, I would have beheaded you with my sword! The Prophet (ﷺ) was looking at Umar in a calm and peaceful manner, and he said: 'O Umar, you should have given us sincere counseling, rather than to do what you did! O Umar, go and repay him his loan, and give him twenty *Sa'a* (measurement of weight) extra because you scared him!'

Zaid said: 'Umar went with me, and repaid me the debt, and gave me over it twenty *Sa'a* of dates. I asked him: 'What is this?' He said: 'The Messenger of God (ﷺ) ordered me to give it, because I frightened you.' Zaid then asked Umar: 'O Umar, do you know who I am?' Umar said: 'No, I don't - who are you?' Zaid said: 'I am Zaid b. Sa'nah.' Umar inquired: 'The Rabbi?' Zaid answered: 'Yes, the Rabbi.' Umar then asked him: 'What made you say what you said to the Prophet (ﷺ) and do what you did to him?' Zaid answered: 'O Umar, I have seen all the signs of prophethood in the face of the Messenger of God (ﷺ) except two – (the first) his patience and perseverance precede his anger and the second, the more harsher you are towards him, the kinder and more patient he becomes, and I am now satisfied. O Umar, I hold you as a witness that I testify and am satisfied that there is no true god worthy of being worshipped except God alone, and my religion is

Islam and Muhammad (ﷺ) is my Prophet. I also hold you as a witness that half of my wealth - and I am among the wealthiest people in Madeenah - I give for the sake of God to the Muslims.' Umar said: 'you will not be able to distribute your wealth to all the Muslims, so say, 'I will distribute it to some of the followers of Muhammad (ﷺ).' Zaid said: 'I said, then I will distribute (the apportioned) wealth to some of the Muslims.' Both Zaid and Umar returned to the Messenger of God (ﷺ). Zaid said to him: 'I bear witness that there is no true god worthy of being worshipped except God alone, and that Muhammad (ﷺ) is the slave of God and His Messenger.' He believed in him, and witnessed many battles and then died in the Battle of Tabook while he was encountering the enemy - may God have mercy on Zaid.' (Ibn Hibban #288)

A great example of his forgiveness and perseverance is apparent when he pardoned the people of Makkah after its conquest. When the Messenger of God (ﷺ) gathered the people; who had abused, harmed and tortured him and his companions, and had driven them out of the city of Makkah, he said:

'What do you think I will do to you?' They answered: 'You will only do something favorable; you are a kind and generous brother, and a kind and generous nephew!' The Prophet (ﷺ) said: 'Go - you are free to do as you wish.' (Baihaqi #18055)

30. Patience: The Messenger of God (ﷺ) was the epitome of patience. He was patient with his people before calling them to Islam; for they would worship idols and do sinful acts. He was patient and tolerant with the abuse and harm the pagans of Makkah inflicted on him and his Companions and sought the reward of God. He was also patient and tolerant with the abuse of the hypocrites in Madeenah.

His patience was severely tested when he lost his loved ones. His wife, Khadeejah, died during his lifetime, as did all his children, save his daughter, Fatimah. His uncle Hamzah and Abu Talib passed away as well. The Prophet (ﷺ) was patient and sought the reward of God. Anas b. Malik said:

'We entered the house of Abu Saif - the blacksmith - with the Prophet (ﷺ). Abu Saif's wife was the wet-nurse of his son, Ibraheem. The Messenger of God (ﷺ) lifted his son Ibraheem, and smelled and kissed him. After a while he went and saw his son again - he was dying. The Prophet (ﷺ) started to cry. Abdur-rahmaan b. Auf said: 'O Prophet of God, you too cry!' The Messenger (ﷺ) said: 'O Ibn Auf, this is a mercy' - the Prophet (ﷺ) shed more tears and said: 'The eyes shed tears, the heart is saddened, and we only say what pleases our Lord, and we are saddened by your death, O Ibraheem!' (Bukhari #1241)

31. **Justice and Fairness:** The Messenger of God (ﷺ) was just and fair in every aspect of his life and in the application of the religion. A'ishah said:

'The people of Quraish were extremely concerned about a Makhzoomi woman (i.e. the woman from the tribe of Makhzoom) who committed a theft. They conversed among themselves and said, 'Who can intercede on her behalf with the Messenger of God (ﷺ)?'

They finally said: 'Who dares to speak to the Messenger of God (ﷺ) in this matter except Usamah b. Zaid, the most beloved young man to the Messenger of God (ﷺ).' So Usamah spoke to the Messenger of God (ﷺ) regarding the woman. The Messenger of God (ﷺ) said:

'O Usamah! Do you intercede (on their behalf to disregard) one of God's castigations and punishments!'

The Messenger of God (ﷺ) got up and delivered a speech, saying:

'People before you were destroyed because when the noble among them stole, they would let him go; and if the poor and weak stole they would punish him. By God! If Fatimah, the daughter of Muhammad stole, I would cut her hand off.' (Bukhari #3288)

The Messenger of God (ﷺ) was just and fair and allowed others to avenge themselves if he harmed them. Usaid b. Hudhair said:

'A man from the Ansar, was cracking jokes with people and making them laugh, and the Prophet (ﷺ)

55

passed by him and poked his side lightly with a branch of a tree that he was carrying. The man exclaimed: 'O Prophet of God! Allow me to avenge myself!' The Prophet (ﷺ) said: 'Go Ahead!' The man said: 'O Messenger of God, you are wearing a garment, and I was not when you poked me [i.e. you jabbed my exposed skin, so it is only fair I do the same to you]!' The Messenger of God (ﷺ) raised his upper garment [to expose his side], and the Ansari [merely] kissed it, saying: 'I only meant to do this, O Messenger of God!'   (Abu Dawood #5224)

32. Fearing God, and Being Mindful of Him: The Messenger of God (ﷺ) was the most mindful person of God. Abdullah bin Masoud said:

'[Once] the Messenger of God (ﷺ) said to me: 'Recite to me from the Qur'an!' Abdullah b. Masood said: 'Shall I recite it to you, while it was you to whom it was revealed?!' The Prophet (ﷺ) said: 'Yes.' He said: 'I started to recite Surat an-Nisaa[23], until I reached the verse:

❮How then if We brought from each nation a witness, and We brought you as a witness against these people!❯ (4:41)

Upon hearing this verse, the Messenger of God (ﷺ) said: 'That is enough!' Abdullah b. Masood said, 'I

---

[23] The fourth chapter of the Qur'an.

turned around and saw the Messenger of God (ﷺ) crying.' " (Bukhari #4763)

A'ishah said:

'If the Messenger of God (ﷺ) saw dark clouds in the sky; he would pace forwards and backwards and would exit and enter his house. As soon as it rained, the Prophet (ﷺ) would relax. A'ishah asked him about it, and he said: 'I do not know, it may be as some people said:

❮Then, when they saw the (penalty in the shape of) a cloud traversing the sky, coming to meet their valleys, they said: 'This cloud will give us rain! Nay, it is the (calamity) you were asking to be hastened! A wind wherein is a Grievous Penalty!❯[24] **(46:24)**

33. Richness and Contentment of the Heart: Umar b. al-Khattab said:

'I entered the Messenger's house and I found him sitting on a mat. He had a leather pillow stuffed with fibers. He had a pot of water by his feet, and there was some clothes hung on the wall. His side had marks due to the mat that he lay on. Umar wept when he saw this, and the Messenger (ﷺ) asked him: 'Why do you weep?' Umar said: 'O Prophet of God! Khosrau and Caesar enjoy the best of this world, and you are suffering in poverty?!' He said: 'Aren't you pleased that they enjoy this world, and we will enjoy the Hereafter?' (Bukhari #4629)

---

[24] Bukhari #3034.

34. Hoping for Goodness, Even for his Enemies: A'ishah said:

'I asked the Messenger of God (⁂): "Did you face a day harder and more intense than the Battle of Uhud?" He replied: 'I suffered a lot from your people! The worst I suffered was on the Day of al-'Aqabah when I spoke to Ali b. Abd Yaleel b. Abd Kilaal (in order to support me) but he disappointed me and left me. I left the area while I was quite worried, and walked - when I reached an area called *Qarn ath-Tha'alib*, I raised my head to the sky and noticed a cloud that shaded me. Gabriel (⁂) called me and said: 'O Muhammad! God, the Exalted, has heard what your people have said to you - and has sent the Angel in charge of the mountains, so you can command him to do what you please.' The Prophet (⁂) said: 'The Angel in charge of the mountains called me saying: 'May God praise you and keep safe from all evil! O Muhammad, I will do whatever you command me to do. If you like I can bring the *Akhshabain* mountains together and crush them all.' The Messenger of God (⁂) said: 'It may be that God raises from among them a progeny who worship God alone and associate no partners with Him.' (Bukhari #3059)

The Prophet's Manners with His Companions

1. **The Prophet's close relations with his Companions**: The Prophet was very close to his companions, and this is well-known when one reads the detailed reports about the Prophet's biography. The Prophet (ﷺ) is the example which we should emulate in all our matters. Jareer b. Abdullah said: 'The Prophet (ﷺ) did not prevent me from sitting with him since I accepted Islam. He always smiled when he looked at me. I once complained to him that I could not ride a horse and he hit me in my chest and supplicated God, saying:

'O God! Steady him, and make him a person who guides others and a source of guidance.' (Bukhari #5739)

2. **The Prophet (ﷺ) would entertain his Companions and joke with them**: Al-Hasan said: 'An old woman came to the Prophet (ﷺ) and said: "O Messenger of God, ask God to admit me into the Heavenly Gardens." He said: "Old women will not enter the Heavenly Gardens!" She then walked away crying. The Prophet (ﷺ) said: "Tell her that she will not enter the Heavenly Gardens as an old woman, for Allah says:

❴Verily, We have created them (maidens) of special creation. And made them virgins. Loving (their husbands only), (and) of equal age.❵ [56:35-7]

The Prophet (ﷺ) did not only verbally entertain and joke with his companions, but sported and amused them as well. Anas b. Malik said:

'A Bedouin named Zahir b. Haram would give gifts to the Prophet (ﷺ) and he would prepare things for him as well. The Prophet (ﷺ) said: **'Zahir is our desert, and we are his city.'**

The Prophet (ﷺ) approached him while he was selling his goods, and the Prophet (ﷺ) hugged him from behind, and he could not see him. He then said: 'Let me go!' When he knew that it was the Prophet (ﷺ) who was hugging him, he pressed his back towards the Messenger's chest! The Messenger of God (ﷺ) then said: 'Who will buy this slave from me?' Zahir said: 'O Messenger of God, I am worthless!' The Messenger of God ﷺ said:

'You are not considered worthless by God!' or he said: **'You are valuable and precious to God.'** (Ibn Hibban #5790)

3. **He would consult his Companions**: The Prophet (ﷺ) would consult his Companions, and take their opinions and points of view into consideration in issues and matters for which no textual proofs were revealed. Abu Hurairah said:

'I have not seen a person more keen for the sincere advice of his companions than the Messenger of God (ﷺ).' (Tirmidthi #1714)

4. **Visiting the sick, whether he was Muslim or non-Muslim**: The Prophet (ﷺ) was concerned about his Com-

panions and would make sure that they were well. If he was told about a Companion who was sick, he would rush to visit him with the Companions that were present with him. He wouldn't only visit the Muslims who were sick; rather, he would even visit non-Muslims. Anas b. Malik said:

'A Jewish boy would serve the Prophet (ﷺ) and he fell sick, so the Prophet (ﷺ) said: 'Let us go and visit him.' They went to visit him, and found his father sitting by his head, and the Messenger of God (ﷺ) said: 'proclaim that there is no true god worthy of being worshipped except Allah alone' and I will intercede on your behalf on account of it on the Day of Resurrection.' The boy looked at his father, and the father said: 'Obey Abul-Qasim![25]' so the boy uttered: 'There is no true god worthy of being worshipped except Allah alone and Muhammad (ﷺ) is the last Messenger.' The Messenger of God (ﷺ) said: 'All praise is due to God, Who saved him from the Fire of Hell.' (Ibn Hibban #2960)

5. He was grateful for people's goodness towards him, and would reward that generously: Abdullah b. Umar said that the Messenger of God (ﷺ) said:

'Whoever seeks refuge with God against your evil, then do not harm him. Whoever asks you by God, then give him. Whoever invites you, then accept his invitation. Whoever does a favor for you or an act of

---

[25] Another name of the Prophet (ﷺ).

kindness, then repay him in a similar manner; but if you do not find that which you can reward him with, then supplicate God for him continuously, until you think you have repaid him.' (Ahmed #6106)

A'ishah said:

'The Messenger of God (ﷺ) would accept gifts, and reward generously on account of that.' (Bukhari #2445)

6. The Messenger's love for everything which is beautiful and good: Anas said:

'The hand of the Messenger of God (ﷺ) was softer than any silk that I had ever touched, and his scent was sweeter than any perfume that I had ever smelt.' (Bukhari #3368)

7. The Messenger of God (ﷺ) loved to help others by interceding on their behalf:

Abdullah b. Abbas said:

'The husband of Bareerah was a slave whose name was Mugheeth - I saw him walking behind her in the streets of Madeenah crying, and his tears were falling off his beard. The Messenger of God (ﷺ) said to Al-Abbas: 'Doesn't it amaze you, how much Mugheeth loves Bareerah, and how much she dislikes Mugheeth!'

The Prophet (ﷺ) said to Bareerah: 'Why don't you go back to him?' She said to him: 'Are you commanding me to do so?' He said: 'No, but I am interceding on his behalf.' She said: 'I have no need for him.' (Bukhari # 4875)

8. The Messenger of God (ﷺ) would serve himself:
A'ishah said:

'I was asked how the Messenger of God (ﷺ) behaved
in his house.' She said: 'He was like any man; he
washed his clothes, milked his sheep, and served
himself.' (Ahmed 24998)

The Prophet's excellent manners, not only made him serve
himself; rather, he would serve others as well. A'ishah
said:

'I was asked how the Messenger of God (ﷺ) behaved
in his house.' She said: 'He would help out in the
house with the daily chores, and when he heard the
Adthan he would leave [everything and head] for the
Mosque.' (Bukhari 5048)

Statements of Justice and Equity:

1. **The German Poet, Wolfgang Göethe**[26], said: 'I looked into history for a human paradigm and found it to be in Muhammad 醬.'

2. **Professor Keith Moore**[27], said in his book: *The Developing Human*:

> It is clear to me that these statements must have come to Muhammad from God, or Allah, because most of this knowledge was not discovered until many centuries later. This proves to me that Muhammad must have been a messenger of God, or Allah.

He further said: 'I have no difficulty in my mind reconciling that this is a divine inspiration or revelation, which lead him to these statements.'

3. **Dr. Maurice Bucaille**[28], said in his book: *The Qur'an, and Modern Science*:

> A totally objective examination of it [the Qur'an] in the light of modern knowledge, leads us to recognize the agreement between the two, as has been already noted on repeated occasions. It makes us deem it quite unthinkable for a man of Muhammad's time to have been

---

[26] German writer and scientist. A master of poetry, drama, and the novel. He also conducted scientific research in various fields, notably botany, and held several governmental positions.

[27] He was the former President of the Canadian Association of Anatomists, Department of anatomy and cell biology, University of Toronto.

[28] Dr. Maurice Bucaille was an eminent French surgeon, scientist, scholar and author of "The Bible, The Qur'an and Science."

the author of such statements, on account of the state of knowledge in his day. Such considerations are part of what gives the Qur'anic Revelation its unique place, and forces the impartial scientist to admit his inability to provide an explanation which calls solely upon materialistic reasoning.'

4. **Annie Besant**[29] in *The Life and Teachings of Mohammad*, said:

It is impossible for anyone who studies the life and character of the great Prophet of Arabia, who knew how he taught and how he lived, to feel anything but reverence for the mighty Prophet, one of the great messengers of the Supreme. And although in what I put to you I shall say many things which may be familiar to many, yet I myself feel, whenever I reread them, a new way of admiration, a new sense of reverence for that mighty Arabian teacher.

5. **Dr. Gustav Weil** in *History of the Islamic Peoples* said:

Muhammad was a shining example to his people. His character was pure and stainless. His house, his dress, his food –they were characterized by a rare simplicity. So unpretentious was he that he would receive from his companions no special mark of reverence, nor would he accept any service from his slave which he could do for himself. He was accessible to all at all times. He visited the sick and was full of sympathy for all. Unlimited was

---

[29] English theosophist, philosopher, and political figure who advocated home rule and educational reforms in India.

his benevolence and generosity as also was his anxious care for the welfare of the community.[30]

6. **Maurice Gaudefroy** said:

Muhammad was a prophet, not a theologian, a fact so evident that one is loath to state it. The men who surrounded him and constituted the influential elite of the primate Muslim community, contented themselves with obeying the law that he had proclaimed in the name of Allah and with following his teaching and example.[31]

7. **Washington Irving**[32], said:

His military triumphs awakened no pride nor vain glory as they would have done had they been effected by selfish purposes. In the time of his greatest power he maintained the same simplicity of manner and appearance as in the days of his adversity. So far from affecting regal state, he was displeased if, on entering a room, any unusual testimonial of respect was shown to him.[33]

8. **Edmund Burke** said: "The Muhammadan law, which is binding on all from the crowned head to the meanest subject, is a law interwoven with a system of the wisest, the most learned and the most enlightened jurisprudence that ever existed in the world."[34]

---

[30] Encyclopedia of Seerah, by Afzalur-Rahman.

[31] ibid

[32] He was a famous writer. He died in 1859.

[33] Encyclopedia of Seerah, by Afzalur-Rahman.

[34] ibid

The Wives of the Prophet ﷺ:

After the death of his first wife, Khadeejah, the Prophet (ﷺ) married eleven women; all were divorcees, except for A'ishah. Six of his wives were from the tribe of Quraish, and five were from different Arabian tribes. The Prophet (ﷺ) married these women for a number of reasons:

1. **Religious and legislative purpose:** The Prophet (ﷺ) married Zainab b. Jahsh. The Arabs in the Era of Ignorance would prohibit a man from marrying the wife of his adopted son; they believed that the adopted son was like a man's actual son in all aspects. The Prophet (ﷺ) married her, although she was previously the wife of his adopted son, Zaid b. Harithah. The Messenger of God (ﷺ) married her to abolish this belief. God, the Exalted, says:

❲And when you said to him to whom Allah had shown favor and to whom you had shown a favor: keep your wife to yourself and be careful of (your duty to) Allah; and you concealed in your soul what Allah would bring to light, and you feared men, and Allah had a greater right that you should fear Him. But when Zaid had accomplished his want of her, We gave have her to you as a wife, so that there should be no difficulty for the believers in respect of the wives of their adopted sons, when they have accomplished their want of them; and Allah's command shall be fulfilled..❳ (33:37)

2. **Political reasons and for the spread of Islam, to invite people to Islam, and to gain the favor of the Arab tribes:** The Messenger of God (ﷺ) married women from the largest and strongest Arab tribes. The Prophet (ﷺ) ordered his Companions to do this as well. The Prophet (ﷺ) said to Abdurrahmaan b. Auf:

> 'If they obey you (i.e. accept Islam) then marry the daughter of the head of the tribe.'

Dr. Cahan said: 'Some of the aspects of his life may seem confusing to us due to present day mentality. The Messenger is criticized due to his obsession of attaining worldly desires and his nine wives, whom he married after the death of his wife Khadeejah. It has been confirmed that most of these marriages were for political reasons, which were aimed to gain loyalty of some nobles, and tribes.'

3. **Social reasons:** The Prophet (ﷺ) married some of his Companions' wives who had died, in battle or while on a mission to preach Islam. He married them even though they were older than him, and he did so to honor them and their husbands.

Veccia Vaglieri[35] in her book 'In Defense of Islam' said: 'Throughout the years of his youth, Muhammad (ﷺ) only married one woman, even though the sexuality of man is at its peak during this period. Although he lived in the society he lived in, wherein plural marriage was considered

---

[35] A famous Italian Orientalist.

the general rule, and divorce was very easy - he only married one woman, although she was older than him. He was a faithful husband to her for twenty-five years, and did not marry another woman, except after her death. He at that time was fifty years old. He married each of his wives thereafter for a social or political purpose; such that he wanted to honor the pious women, or wanted the loyalty of certain tribes so that Islam would spread amongst them. All the wives Muhammad (ﷺ) married were not virgin, nor were they young or beautiful; except for A'ishah. So how can anyone claim that he was a lustful man? He was a man not a god. His wish to have a son may have also lead him to marry; for the children that he had from Khadeejah all died. Moreover, who undertook the financial responsibilities of his large family, without having large resources. He was just and fair towards them all and did not differentiate between them at all. He followed the practice of previous Prophets such as Moses, whom no one objected to their plural marriage. Is the reason why people object to the plural marriage of Muhammad (ﷺ) the fact that we know the minute details of his life, and know so little of the details of the lives of the Prophets before him?'

Thomas Carlyle said: 'Mahomet himself, after all that can be said about him, was not a sensual man. We shall err widely if we consider this man as a common voluptuary, intent mainly on base enjoyments,--nay on enjoyments of any kind.'[36]

---

[36] 'Heroes, Hero-Worship and the Heroic in History'

Textual Proofs which support the
Prophethood of Muhammad 鷄

Proofs from the Qur'an:

1. God, the Exalted, says:

❨Muhammad is not the father of any of your men, but (he is) the Messenger of Allah, and the last of the Prophets: and Allah has full knowledge of all things.❩ (33:40)

2. Jesus 鷄 gave the glad tidings of Prophet Muhammad in the Gospel. God, the Exalted, says:

❨And remember, Jesus, the son of Mary, said: "O Children of Israel! I am the Messenger of Allah (sent) to you, confirming the Law (which came) before me, and giving Glad Tidings of a Messenger to come after me, whose name shall be Ahmad." But when he came to them with Clear Signs they said, 'This is evident sorcery!'❩ (61:6)

Proofs from the Sunnah[37]:

The Prophet (鷄) said:

'My example and the example of the Prophets before me is like a man who built a house, which he built

---

[37] Sunnah: the narration of the speech, actions, characteristics, or tacit approvals of the Prophet.

and perfected except for the space of one block; people would go round the house and stare in awe at its perfection and say, 'Had it not been for this space!' The Prophet (ﷺ) said: 'I am that brick, I am the last of Prophets.' (Bukhari #3342)

Previous Scriptures:

Ataa' b. Yasaar, said: 'I met Abdullah b. Amr b. al-Aas and I asked him:

'Tell me about the description of the Messenger of God (ﷺ) in the Torah.' He said: 'He is described in the Torah with some of what he is described in the Qur'an; 'We have indeed sent you as a witness (over mankind) and one who gives glad-tidings, and warns others, and one who protects and safeguards the commoners. You are My slave and Messenger; I called you *Mutawakkil* (The Trusted One). You are neither ill-mannered nor rude, nor do you raise your voice. You do not pay evil with evil; rather, you forgive and pardon. I will not collect his soul until I guide the nations, and until they say, 'There is no true god worthy of being worshipped except God alone' and until they clearly see the Truth.'

Ata said: I met Ka'b, the Rabbi, and asked him about this narration, and he did not differ with Abdullah b. Amr b. Al-Aas except for a minor difference in the wording of the narration.' (Baihaqi #13079)

Abdul-Ahad Dawud[38], said: 'but I have tried to base my arguments on portions of the Bible which hardly allow of any linguistic dispute. I would not go to Latin, Greek, or Aramaic, for that would be useless: I just give the following quotation in the very words of the Revised Version as published by the British and Foreign Bible Society.

We read the following words in the Book of Deuteronomy chapter xviii. verse 18: "I will raise them up a prophet from among their brethren, like unto thee; and I will put my words in his mouth." If these words do not apply to Prophet Muhammad, they still remain unfulfilled. Prophet Jesus himself never claimed to be the Prophet alluded to. Even his disciples were of the same opinion: they looked to the second coming of Jesus for the fulfillment of the prophecy. So far it is undisputed that the first coming of Jesus was not the advent of the "prophet like unto thee," and his second advent can hardly fulfill the words. Jesus, as is believed by his Church, will appear as a Judge and not as a law-giver; but the promised one has to come with a "fiery law" in "his right hand."

In ascertaining the personality of the promised prophet the other prophecy of Moses is, however, very helpful where it speaks of the shining forth of God from Paran, the mountain of Mecca. The words in the Book of Deuteronomy, chapter xxxiii. verse 2, run as follows: "The Lord came from Sinai, and rose up from Seir unto them; he shined forth from mount Paran, and he came with ten

---

[38] He was Rev. David Benjamin Keldani, B.D. A Roman Catholic priest of the Uniate-Chaldean sect. He was born in 1867 at Urmia in Persia.

thousands of saints; from his right hand went a fiery law for them."

In these words the Lord has been compared with the sun. He comes from Sinai, he rises from Seir, but he shines in his full glory from Paran, where he had to appear with ten thousands of saints with a fiery law in his right hand. None of the Israelites, including Jesus, had anything to do with Paran. Hagar, with her son Ishmael, wandered in the wilderness of Beersheba, who afterwards dwelt in the wilderness of Paran (Gen. xxi. 21). He married an Egyptian woman, and through his first-born, Kedar, gave descent to the Arabs who from that time till now are the dwellers of the wilderness of Paran. And if Prophet Muhammad admittedly on all hands traces his descent to Ishmael through Kedar and he appeared as a prophet in the wilderness of Paran and reentered Mecca with ten thousand saints and gave a fiery law to his people, is not the prophecy above-mentioned fulfilled to its very letter?

The words of the prophecy in Habakkuk are especially noteworthy. His (the Holy One from Paran) glory covered the heavens and the earth was full of his praise. The word "praise" is very significant, as the very name Muhammad literally means "the praised one." Besides the Arabs, the inhabitants of the wilderness of Paran had also been promised a Revelation: "Let the wilderness and the cities thereof lift up their voice, the villages that Kedar doth inhabit: let the inhabitants of the rock sing, let them shout from the top of the mountains. Let them give glory unto the Lord, and declare His praise in the islands. The Lord shall go forth as a mighty man, he shall stir up jealousy like a man of war, he shall cry, yea, roar; he shall prevail against his enemies" (Isaiah).

In connection with it there are two other prophecies worthy of note where references have been made to Kedar. The one runs thus in chapter 1x. of Isaiah: "Arise, shine for thy light is come, and the glory of the Lord is risen upon thee ... The multitude of camels shall cover thee, the dromedaries of Midian and Ephah; all they from Sheba shall come.. All the flocks of Kedar shall be gathered together unto thee, the rams of Nebaioth shall minister unto thee: they shall come up with acceptance on mine altar, and I will glorify the house of my glory" (1-7). The other prophecy is again in Isaiah "The burden upon Arabia. In the forest in Arabia shall ye lodge, O ye travelling companies of Dedanim. The inhabitants of the land of Tema brought water to him that was thirsty, they prevented with their bread him that fled. For they fled from the swords and from the bent bow, and from the grievousness of war. For thus hath the Lord said unto me, Within a year, according to the years of an hireling, and all the glory of Kedar shall fail: And the residue of the number of archers, the mighty of the children of Kedar, shall be diminished" Read these prophecies in Isaiah in the light of one in Deuteronomy which speaks of the shining forth of God from Paran.

If Ishmael inhabited the wilderness of Paran, where he gave birth to Kedar, who is the ancestor of the Arabs; and if the sons of Kedar had to receive revelation from God; if the flocks of Kedar had to come up with acceptance to a Divine altar to glorify "the house of my glory" where the darkness had to cover the earth for some centuries, and then that very land had to receive light from God; and if all the glory of Kedar had to fail and the number of archers, the mighty men of the children of Kedar, had to diminish within a year after the one fled from the swords and from the bent bows - the Holy One from Paran (Habakkuk iii 3) is no one else than Prophet Muhammad. Prophet Muhammad is the holy offspring of Ishmael through Kedar, who settled in the wilderness of Paran. Muhammad is the only Prophet through whom the Arabs received revelation at the time when the darkness had covered the earth.

Through him God shone from Paran, and Mecca is the only place where the House of God is glorified and the flocks of Kedar come with acceptance on its altar. Prophet Muhammad was persecuted by his people and had to leave Mecca. He was thirsty and fled from the drawn sword and the bent bow, and within a year after his flight the descendants of Kedar meet him at Badr, the place of the first battle between the Meccans and the Prophet, the children of Kedar and their number of archers diminish and all the glory of Kedar fails. If the Holy Prophet is not to be accepted as the fulfillment of all these prophecies they will still remain unfulfilled. "The house of my glory" referred to in Isaiah IX is the house of God in Mecca and not the Church of Christ as thought by Christian commentators. The flocks of Kedar, as mentioned in verse 7, have never come to the Church of Christ; and it is a fact that the villages of Kedar and their inhabitants are the only people in the whole world who have remained impenetrable to any influence of the Church of Christ.

Again, the mention of 10,000 saints in Deuteronomy xxx 3 is very significant. He (God) shined forth from Paran, and he came with 10,000 of saints. Read the whole history of the wilderness of Paran and you will find no other event but when Mecca was conquered by the Prophet. He comes with 10,000 followers from Medina and re-enters "the house of my glory." He gives the fiery law to the world, which reduced to ashes all other laws. The Comforter - the Spirit of Truth - spoken of by Prophet Jesus was no other than Prophet Muhammad himself. It cannot be taken as the Holy Ghost, as the Church theology says. "It is expedient for you that I go away," says Jesus, "for if I go not away the Comforter will not come unto you, but if I depart I will send him unto you."

The words clearly show that the Comforter had to come after the departure of Jesus, and was not with him when he uttered these words. Are we to presume that Jesus was devoid of the Holy Ghost if his coming was conditional on the going of Jesus: besides, the way in which Jesus describes him makes him a human being, not a ghost. "He shall not speak of himself, but whatsoever he shall hear that he shall speak." Should we presume that the Holy Ghost and God are two distinct entities and that the Holy Ghost speaks of himself and also what he hears from God? The words of Jesus clearly refer to some messenger from God. He calls him the Spirit of Truth, and so the Koran speaks of Prophet Muhammad, "No, indeed, he has brought the truth, and confirmed the Messengers." Ch.37:37 [39]

Proofs from the New Testament

There are a number of passages in the New Testament which clearly refer to the coming of Muhammad (ﷺ) by implication through the nature of his actions or functions.

*John, the Baptist: The Jews sent priests to him to find out who he was. 'He confessed, "I am not the Christ." And they asked him, "What then? Are you Elijah?" And He said: "I am not." Are you that *Prophet*?' And he answered, "No"…And they said to him: "Why do you baptize then, if you are not the Christ, nor Elijah, nor that *Prophet*?'(John 1:20-25).

That Prophet is not Jesus, but Muhammad, because John the Baptist continued preaching and baptizing and fore-telling the coming of that *Prophet* during the life-time of Jesus.

*Jesus: The Prophet Jesus foretold the coming of another Prophet, whose name would be 'Periqlytos' or 'Paraclete' or 'Paracalon' and who (that is, whose teaching) would last forever, 'I will pray the Father, and He shall give you another Comforter (Periqlytos), that he may abide with you forever.' (John XIV, 16).

---

[39] Muhammad in the Bible, Abdul-Ahad Dawud.

The word periqlytos means 'illustrious, 'renowned' and 'praiseworthy' and this is exactly what the name 'Ahmed' means. It is confirmed in the Qur'an that the Prophet Jesus did prophesize that a Prophet named 'Ahmed' would come after him. God, the Exalted, says:

⦃And remember when Jesus the son of Mary, said: "O Children of Israel! I am the Messenger of Allah unto you, confirming the Torah which came before me, and giving glad tidings of a Messenger to come after me, whose name shall be Ahmed.⦄ (61:6)

Intellectual Proofs of His Prophethood

1. **The Prophet (ﷺ) was unlettered.** He did not know how to read or write. He lived among a people who were unlettered as well. Therefore one cannot claim that the Qur'an was authored by Muhammad (ﷺ)! God, the Exalted, says:

❨And you did not recite any Book before it, nor did you write one with your right hand; in that case the liars would have doubted.❩ (29:48)

2. **The Arabs were challenged to bring forth something similar to the Qur'an, and they were unable to do so!** The beauty, structure and deep meanings of the Qur'an amazed the Arabs. The Qur'an is the everlasting miracle of Muhammad (ﷺ). The Messenger of God (ﷺ) said:

'The miracles of the Prophets (before Muhammad ﷺ) were confined to their times. The miracle I have been given is the Qur'an, which is everlasting; therefore, I hope to have the most followers.' (Bukhari 4598)

Even though his people were eloquent and well known for their awesome poetry, God challenged them to produce similar to the Qur'an, but they couldn't. God then challenged them to produce a chapter similar to it, and they couldn't.

God says:

❨And if you are in doubt as to what We have sent down to Our slave, then produce a chapter like it, and call upon your helpers beside Allah, if you are truthful.❭ (2:23)

God challenges mankind at large to bring forth similar to the Qur'an. God says:

❬Say, 'if mankind and the Jinn gathered together to produce the like of this Qur'an, they could not produce the like thereof, even though they should help one another.❭ (17:88)

3. The Prophet ﷺ continued preaching and calling people to Islam, even though he faced many hardships and was confronted by his people, who were plotting to kill him. Yet the Prophet ﷺ continued preaching, and was patient. If he was an imposter - he would stop preaching and would have feared for his life.

W. Montgomery Watt said:

His readiness to undergo persecution for his beliefs, the high moral character of the men who believed in him and looked up to him as a leader, and the greatness of his ultimate achievement - all argue his fundamental integrity. To suppose Muhammad an impostor raises more problems that it solves. Moreover, none of the great figures of history is so poorly appreciated in the West as Muhammad.... Thus, not merely must we credit Muhammad with essential honesty and integrity of purpose, if we are to understand him at all; if we are to correct the errors we have inherited from the past, we must not forget the conclusive proof is a much stricter requirement than a show of plausibility, and in a matter such as this only to be attained with difficulty.

4. Every person loves the ornaments and beauties of this life, and would be swayed by these things. God, the Exalted, says:

❲Beautified for men is the love of desired things – women and children, and stored-up heaps of gold and silver, and pastured horses and cattle and crops. That is the provision of the present life; but it is God with Whom is an excellent abode.❳ (3:14)

Man, by his nature, is keen in acquiring ornaments and beauties of this world. People differ in the method they use to acquire these things. Some would resort to using lawful means to gain these things, while others would resort to using unlawful means to acquire these things.

If this is known (you should know that) Quraish tried to persuade the Prophet (☻) to stop calling people to Islam. They told him that they would make him the master of Quraish, marry him to the most beautiful women, and make him the most affluent man amongst them. He responded to these tempting offers, saying:

'By God, if they place the sun in my right hand, and the moon in my left hand to leave this matter, I would not leave it, until God makes it apparent, or I am killed calling people to it.' (Ibn Hisham)

Were the Prophet ☻ an impostor he would have accepted this offer without hesitation.

Thomas Carlyle, said:

They called him a prophet, you say? Why, he stood there face to face with them, here, not enshrined in any mystery, visibly clouting his own cloak, cobbling his own shoes, fighting, counseling ordering in the midst of them. They must have seen what kind of a man he was, let him be called what ye like. No emperor with his tiaras was obeyed as this man in a cloak of his own clouting. During three and twenty ears of rough, actual trial, I find something of a veritable hero necessary for that of itself.[40]

5. **It is well known that subjects and wealth of a kingdom are subjected to the will of the king, and his service.** As for Muhammad (ﷺ) he knew that this life was a transitory stage. Ibraheem b. Alqamah said that Abdullah said: 'The Prophet (ﷺ) lay down on a straw mat which had marked his side, so I said: 'O Messenger of God! I ransom you with my mother and father! Allow us to put bedding on this mat that you lay on, so your side would not be affected and marked.' The Prophet (ﷺ) said:

'My example in this life is like a rider who took rest under the shade of a tree then continued on his journey.' (Ibn Majah #4109)

An-Nu'man b. Basheer said:

'I saw your Prophet (ﷺ) (during a time) when he was not able to even find low quality dates to fill his stomach.' (Muslim #2977)

---

[40] 'Heroes, Hero-Worship and the Heroic in History'

Abu Hurairah said:

'The Messenger of God (ﷺ) never filled his stomach for three consecutive days until his death.' (Bukhari #5059)

Even though the Arabian Peninsula was under his control, and he was the source of goodness for its people, the Prophet (ﷺ) would at some times not find food to suffice him. His wife, A'ishah said that the Prophet (ﷺ) bought some food from a Jew (and agreed to pay him at a later time) and he gave him his armor as collateral.' (Bukhari #2088)

This does not mean that he could not obtain what he wanted; for the moneys and wealth would be placed in front of him in his Masjid, and he would not move from his spot, until he distributed it amongst the poor and needy. Among his Companions were those who were wealthy and affluent - they would rush to serve him and would give up the most valuable of things for him. The reason the Prophet (ﷺ) renounced the riches of this world, was because he knew the reality of this life. He said: 'The likeness of this world to the Hereafter, is like a person who dipped his finger in the ocean - let him see what would return.' (Muslim #2858)

Reverend Bosworth Smith said:

If ever a man ruled by a right divine, it was Muhammad, for he had all the powers without their supports.

He cared not for the dressings of power. The simplicity of his private life was in keeping with his public life.[41]

6. **Certain incidents would befall the Prophet of God (ﷺ) which would need clarification, and he would not be able to do anything because he did not receive revelation regarding it.** During this period (i.e. between the incident and revelation) he would be exhausted. One such incident is the incident of *Ifk*[42] wherein the Prophet's wife A'ishah was accused of being treacherous. The Prophet (ﷺ) did not receive revelation concerning this incident for one month; during which his enemies talked ill of him, until revelation was revealed and the innocence of A'ishah was declared. Were the Prophet (ﷺ) an imposter he would have resolved this incident the minute it came about. God says:

❨Nor does he speak out of desire.❩ (53:3)

7. **The Prophet (ﷺ) did not ask people to adulate him.** On the contrary, the Prophet (ﷺ) would not be pleased if a person adulated him in any way. Anas said:

'There was no individual more beloved to the Companions than the Messenger of God.' He said: 'If they saw him, they would not stand up for him, because they knew he disliked that.' (Tirmidthi #2754)

---

[41] Muhammad and Muhammadanism.

[42] i.e. The incident wherein the hypocrites falsely accused A'ishah, with whom Allah is pleased, of being unchaste.

Washington Irving, said: 'His military triumphs awakened no pride nor vain glory as they would have done had they been effected by selfish purposes. In the time of his greatest power he maintained the same simplicity of manner and appearance as in the days of his adversity. So far from affecting regal state, he was displeased if, on entering a room, any unusual testimonial of respect was shown to him.'

8. **Some verses from the Qur'an were revealed in which the Prophet (ﷺ) was blamed and admonished,** due to some incident or happening; such as:

a. The words of God, the Exalted:

❨**O Prophet! Why do you forbid (for yourself) that which God has allowed to you, seeking to please your wives? And God is Oft-Forgiving, Most Merciful.**❩ (66:1)

The Prophet (ﷺ) abstained from eating honey, due to the behavior of some of his wives. God then admonished him because he forbade upon himself what God deemed lawful.

b. God, the Exalted, says:

❨**May God forgive you (O Muhammad). Why did you grant them leave (for remaining behind; you should have persisted as regards your order to them to proceed on Jihad) until those who told the truth were seen by you in a clear light, and you had known the liars?**❩ (9:43)

God admonished the Prophet (ﷺ) because he quickly accepted the false excuses of the hypocrites who lagged behind in the Battle of Tabook. He forgave them and accepted their excuses, without verifying them.

c. God, the Exalted, says:

❰It is not for a Prophet that he should have prisoners of war (and free them with ransom) until he had made a great slaughter (among his enemies) in the land. You desire the good of this world, but God desires for you the Hereafter. And God is All-Mighty, All-Wise.❱ (8:67)

d. God, the Exalted, says:

❰Not for you (O Muhammad, but for God) is the decision; whether He turns in mercy, to (pardon) them or punishes them; verily, they are the wrong-doers.❱ (3:128)

e. God, the Exalted, says:

❰The Prophet frowned and turned away. Because there came to him the blind man. And how can you know that he might become pure from sins? Or he might receive admonition, and the admonition might profit him?❱ (80:1-4)

Abdullah b. Umm Maktoom, who was blind, came to the Prophet (ﷺ) while he was preaching to one or some of the Quraish leaders, and the Prophet (ﷺ) frowned and turned away - and God admonished him on account of that.

Therefore, were the Prophet (ﷺ) an imposter, these verses would not be found in the Qur'an.

Muhammad Marmaduke Pickthall said:

> One day when the Prophet was in conversation with one of the great men of Qureysh, seeking to persuade him of the truth of Al-Islam, a blind man came and asked him a question concerning the faith. The Prophet was annoyed at the interruption, frowned and turned away from the blind man. In this Surah he is told that a man's importance is not to be judged from his appearance or worldly station.[43]

9. **One of the sure signs of his Prophethood is found in the Chapter of** *Lahab* **(chapter 111) in the Qur'an.** In it God, the Exalted, condemned Abu Lahab (the Prophet's uncle) to the torment of Hell. This chapter was revealed during the early stages of his *Da'wah* (call to Islam). Were the Prophet (ﷺ) an imposter he would not issue a ruling like this; since his uncle might accept Islam afterwards!

Dr. Gary Miller says:

> For example, the Prophet (ﷺ) had an uncle by the name of Abu Lahab. This man hated Islam to such an extent that he used to follow the Prophet around in order to discredit him. If Abu Lahab saw the Prophet (ﷺ) speaking to a stranger, he would wait until they parted and then would go back to the stranger and ask him, 'What did he tell you? Did he say black? Well, it's white. Did he say 'Morning?' Well, it's night.' He faithfully said the ex-

---

[43] The Glorious Qur'an pg. 685

act opposite of whatever he heard Muhammad (ﷺ) say. However, about ten years before Abu Lahab died a little chapter in the Qur'an was revealed to him. It distinctly stated that he would go to the Fire (i.e. Hell). In other words, it affirmed that he would never become a Muslim and would therefore be condemned forever. For ten years all Abu Lahab had to do was say, 'I heard that it has been revealed to Muhammad that I will never change – that I will never become a Muslim and will enter the Hellfire. Well I want to become a Muslim now. How do you like that? What do you think of your divine revelation now?' But he never did that. And yet, that is exactly the kind of behavior one would have expected from him since he always sought to contradict Islam. In essence, Muhammad (ﷺ) said: 'You hate me and you want to finish me? Here, say these words, and I am finished. Come on, say them!' But Abu Lahab never said them. Ten years! And in all that time he never accepted Islam or even became sympathetic to the Islamic cause. How could Muhammad possibly have known for sure that Abu Lahab would fulfill the Qur'anic revelation if he (i.e. Muhammad) was not truly the Messenger of Allah? How could he possibly have been so confident as to give someone ten years to discredit his claim of Prophethood? The only answer is that he was Allah's Messenger; for in order to put forth such a risky challenge, one has to be entirely convinced that he has a divine revelation.[44]

---

[44] The Amazing Qur'an

10. The Prophet (ﷺ) is called: 'Ahmed' in a verse of the Qur'an instead of 'Muhammad'. God, the Exalted, says:

❨And remember when Eesa, son of Maryam said: 'O Children of Israel! I am the Messenger of God unto you, confirming the Torah which came before me, and giving glad tidings of a Messenger to come after me, whose name shall be Ahmed. But when he came to them with clear proofs, they said: 'This is plain magic.'❩ (61:6)

Were he an imposter, the name 'Ahmed' would not have been mentioned in the Qur'an, since he was known as 'Muhammad' amongst his people.

11. **The religion of Islam still exists today and is spreading all over the Globe.** Thousands of people embrace Islam and prefer it over all other religions. This happens even though the callers to Islam are not financially backed as expected; and in spite of the efforts of the enemies of Islam to halt the spread of Islam. God, the Exalted, says:

❨Verily, We sent down the Reminder (i.e. the Qur'an) and surely, We will guard it from corruption.❩ (15:9)

Thomas Carlyle said:

A false man found a religion? Why, a false man cannot build a brick house! If he does not know and follow truly the properties of mortar, burnt clay and what else he works in, it is no house that he makes, but a rubbish-heap. It will not stand for twelve centuries, to lodge a hundred and eighty millions; it will fall straightway. A man must conform himself to Nature's laws, _be_ verily in communion with Nature and the truth of things, or Nature will answer him, No, not at all! Speciosities are specious--ah me!--a Cagliostro, many Cagliostros, prominent world-leaders, do prosper by their quackery, for a day. It is like a forged bank-note; they get it passed out of _their_ worthless hands: others, not they, have to smart for it. Nature bursts up in fire-flames; French Revolutions and such like, proclaiming with terrible veracity that forged notes are forged. But of a Great Man especially, of him I will venture to assert that it is incredible he should have been other than true. It seems to me the primary foundation of him, and of all that can lie in him, this.[45]

The Prophet ﷺ preserved the Qur'an, after God had preserved it in the Books, chests of men generation after generation. Indeed memorizing and reciting it, learning and teaching it are among the things Muslims are very keen on doing, for the Prophet ﷺ said:

'The best of you are those who learn the Qur'an and teach it.' (Bukhari #4639)

Many have tried to add and omit verses from the Qur'an, but they have never been successful; for these mistakes are discovered almost immediately.

As for the Sunnah of the Messenger of God (ﷺ) which is the second source of legislation in Islam, it has been preserved by trustworthy pious men. They spent their lives gathering these traditions, and scrutinizing them to sepa-

---

[45] 'Heroes, Hero-Worship and the Heroic in History'

rate the weak from the authentic; they even clarified which narrations were fabricated. Whoever looks at the books written in the science of Hadeeth will realize this, and that the narrations that are authentic are in fact authentic.

Michael Hart[46] says:

Muhammad founded and promulgated one of the world's great religions[47], and became an immensely effective political leader. Today, thirteen centuries after his death, his influence is still powerful and pervasive.

12. **Veracity and truthfulness of his principles and that they are good and suitable for every time and place.** The results of the application of Islam are clear and well known, which in turn testify that it is indeed a revelation from God. Furthermore, is it not possible for Prophet Muhammad (ﷺ) to be a Prophet, as many Prophets and Messengers were sent before him? If the answer to this query is that there is nothing that prevents this - we then ask, 'why do you reject his Prophethood, and confirm the Prophethood of the Prophets before him?'

13. **Man cannot bring about laws similar to the laws of Islam which deal with every aspect of life, such as transactions, marriage, social conduct, politics, acts of worship and the like.** So, how can an unlettered man bring

---

[46] 'The 100' A ranking of the most influential persons in history.

[47] We believe that Islam is a Divine revelation from Allah, and that Muhammad ﷺ did not found it.

something like this? Isn't this a clear proof and sign of his Prophethood?

14. The Prophet (ﷺ) did not start calling people to Islam until he turned forty years old. His youth had passed and the age in which he should have rest and spend his time leisurely, was the age in which he was commissioned as a Prophet and charged with the dissemination of Islam.

Thomas Carlyle, said:

> It goes greatly against the impostor theory, the fact that he lived in this entirely unexceptionable, entirely quiet and commonplace way, till the heat of his years was done. He was forty before he talked of any mission from Heaven. All his irregularities, real and supposed, date from after his fiftieth year, when the good Kadijah died. All his "ambition," seemingly, had been, hitherto, to live an honest life; his "fame," the mere good opinion of neighbors that knew him, had been sufficient hitherto. Not till he was already getting old, the prurient heat of his life all burnt out, and _peace_ growing to be the chief thing this world could give him, did he start on the "career of ambition;" and, belying all his past character and existence, set up as a wretched empty charlatan to acquire what he could now no longer enjoy! For my share, I have no faith whatever in that.[48]

---

[48] 'Heroes, Hero-Worship and the Heroic in History'

Conclusion

We conclude this research with the words of Alphonse de LaMartaine[49] in 'Historie de al Turquie':

Never has a man set for himself, voluntarily or involuntarily, a more sublime aim, since this aim was superhuman; to subvert superstitions which had been imposed between man and his Creator, to render God unto man and man unto God; to restore the rational and sacred idea of divinity amidst the chaos of the material and disfigured gods of idolatry, then existing. Never has a man undertaken a work so far beyond human power with so feeble means, for he (Muhammad) had in the conception as well as in the execution of such a great design, no other instrument than himself and no other aid except a handful of men living in a corner of the desert. Finally, never has a man accomplished such a huge and lasting revolution in the world, because in less than two centuries after its appearance, Islam, in faith and in arms, reigned over the whole of Arabia, and conquered, in God's name, Persia Khorasan, Transoxania, Western India, Syria, Egypt, Abyssinia, all the known continent of Northern Africa, numerous islands of the Mediterranean Sea, Spain, and part of Gaul. "If greatness of purpose, smallness of means, and astonishing results are the three criteria of a human genius, who could dare compare any

---

[49] He was a poet, a member of the provisional government, and a one-time presidential candidate.

great man in history with Muhammad? The most famous men created arms, laws, and empires only. They founded, if anything at all, no more than material powers which often crumbled away before their eyes. This man moved not only armies, legislations, empires, peoples, dynasties, but millions of men in one-third of the then inhabited world; and more than that, he moved the altars, the gods, the religions, the ideas, the beliefs and the souls. "On the basis of a Book, every letter which has become law, he created a spiritual nationality which blends together peoples of every tongue and race. He has left the indelible characteristic of this Muslim nationality the hatred of false gods and the passion for the One and Immaterial God. This avenging patriotism against the profanation of Heaven formed the virtue of the followers of Muhammad; the conquest of one-third the earth to the dogma was his miracle; or rather it was not the miracle of man but that of reason. "The idea of the unity of God, proclaimed amidst the exhaustion of the fabulous theogonies, was in itself such a miracle that upon it's utterance from his lips it destroyed all the ancient temples of idols and set on fire one-third of the world. His life, his meditations, his heroic reveling against the superstitions of his country, and his boldness in defying the furies of idolatry, his firmness in enduring them for fifteen years in Mecca, his acceptance of the role of public scorn and almost of being a victim of his fellow countrymen: all these and finally, his flight, his incessant preaching, his wars against odds, his faith in his success and his superhuman security in misfortune, his forbearance in victory, his ambition, which was entirely devoted to one idea and in no manner striving for an empire; his endless prayers, his mystic conversations with God, his death and his triumph after death; all these attest not to an imposture but to a firm conviction which gave him the power to restore a dogma. This dogma was twofold the unity of God and the immateriality of God: the former telling what God is, the latter telling what God is not; the one overthrowing false gods with the sword, the other starting an idea with words. "Philosopher, Orator, Apostle, Legislator, Conqueror of Ideas, Restorer of Rational beliefs....The founder of twenty terrestrial empires and of one spiritual empire that is Muhammad. As regards all standards by which human greatness may be measured, we may well ask, is there any man greater than he?'

الحمد لله رب العالمين

وصلى الله وسلم على نبينا محمد وآله وسلم

All Praise is due to Allah alone, the Lord of the Worlds

And may God praise His Prophet and his household, and keep him safe from all evil.

If you would like to receive more information about Islam, do not hesitate to contact us:

1) Email:

en@islamland.org

2) You may also visit the following sites:

www.islamland.org

www.islamreligion.com

www.islam-guide.com

www.missionislam.com

www.sultan.org

www.islamtoday.com